Spiritual Prepping for the Rapture

~

Sharon L. Clemens

FARM GROVE PUBLISHING

GROVELAND, ILLINOIS

"He who testifies to these things says, 'Surely I am coming quickly.'

Amen. Even so, come, Lord Jesus!"

Revelation 22:20

Cover Art

Kelly Kuczkowski

Introduction

We are all preppers to some extent. We buy fire insurance, life insurance and health insurance and try to keep an emergency fund in savings. Wise investment of what God provides financially is as much preparing for unforeseen circumstances as stocking emergency food and water. But the Lord cautions us not to set our hearts upon earthly treasures to save us. Our faith must be in God, not our stockpile. Our Lord commends those who wisely invest the time, talents, gifts and resources He gives them, saying, "Well done good and faithful servant..." [Matthew 25:14-30] He wants our investments to be profitable, not only spiritually but materially. We are told to be wise concerning the times, doing the work of Christ until He comes, not presuming upon His provision. [Luke 19:13]

Spiritual Prepping for the Rapture offers a spiritual perspective to those preparing for inevitable catastrophe. A spiritual approach to what prophecy students call the end of the end times is the only option that guarantees real security. No amount of stockpiling of food, water, money or gold can prevent an enemy with superior forces from taking all we have.

Our Lord said, "Do not lay up for yourselves treasures on earth, where moth and rust destroy and where thieves break in and steal; but lay up for yourselves treasures in heaven, where neither moth nor rust destroys and where thieves do not break in and steal. For where your treasure is, there your heart will be also." [Matthew 6:19-21] Trusting in earthly treasures creates a weakness in our defenses.

So where does practical prepping end and faith begin? It is not a question of one or the other. As the Lord leads, we use what He has given to us wisely, both to provide for our families and to further the work of Christ. Faith in Christ is inherent in every practical decision we make. "Trust in the LORD with all your heart, and lean not on your own understanding; in all your ways acknowledge Him, and He shall direct your paths." [Proverbs 3:5-6] The spiritual prepper maximizes his full potential because faith is the salt sprinkled on the Christian life making everything savory. Christ, the object of our faith, directs all we do enabling us to exist in a productive and satisfying way.

The best example of how spiritual prepping walks in shoe leather is how the Lord prepared Israel to "bug out" of Egypt and take the wilderness walk to the promised land. He did not tell them to leave Egypt with only the clothes on their backs. Pharaoh was so eager for Israel to leave after the death angel ravished Egypt's first-born that he told Moses to take their flocks and their herds with them. Before this, Pharaoh refused to give Moses any concessions. The Egyptians also urged the people to leave quickly, terrified at what their God would do next.

Exodus 12:35-36 - "Now the children of Israel had done according to the word of Moses, and they had asked from the Egyptians articles of silver, articles of gold, and clothing. And the LORD had given the people favor in the sight of the Egyptians, so that they granted them what they requested. Thus they plundered the Egyptians."

The people of Israel were slaves in Egypt; but when they left, they were weighted down with wealth. They even took their unleavened dough in dough bowls with them on their shoulders. Israel left well-stocked for the wilderness journey, no doubt trading with caravans and nomadic tribes along the way. But the people began grumbling when their provisions grew scarce. In spite of their poor attitudes, God supernaturally provided manna and quail and water from a rock. Earthly provisions can fail. God's power will not.

The Bible teaches Christ followers to be wise, which includes a practical approach to living on the home front. One of my boards on Pinterest is devoted to "The Frugal Cottage Lifestyle." It is filled with advice on cooking, canning, gardening, repurposing, and old-fashion methods. I am not so stuck in another century that I would willingly part with my microwave but I have lived long enough to know that tried and true methods still work if modern conveniences like electricity fail. As preppers say, it is wise to have a back-up plan.

Proverbs is filled with applications of good common sense based on Christian principles. An example of the definitive prepper is the Proverbs 31 woman. She sews and cooks from scratch, sets a good table, manages her household staff, invests in real estate, stays in shape, burns the midnight oil, donates time and money to the poor, dresses herself and her family well, and she operates a cottage industry, in her spare time. In all this she displays virtues of strength, honor, submission and faith.

This woman successfully maintains her daily life but what about the uncertainty of the future? It is the unknown that tests us and she does not fail. In Proverbs 31:25-26, she rejoices in the time to come—she has no fear of the future because as a practicing woman of faith, she is prepared for whatever comes. She is an example of a woman whose spiritual prepping and practical prepping set her apart as a wise steward of her home. This woman is known for her wisdom and for her kindness; her opinion is valued by her family. It is no wonder she is honored by her children and her husband.

In *Spiritual Prepping for the Rapture,* I speak personally about what to expect in the future according to the prophetic Word and how to prepare for it to bring glory to God. Through Christ and His Holy Spirit, we have access into all truth. For the believer, there is no fear of the unknown. [John 16:13]

Spiritual prepping also trains us to access the peace that is available only in Christ—a peace that surpasses human understanding and a hope that will not fail. He told His disciples that in this life we will have tribulation and trials; life is challenging even now in the time preceding the great Tribulation. The good news is that He has overcome the world— if we allow Him to do so. [John 16:33] In dealing with the prime directive, I will also share a bit about my practical Christian life, seeking to be the kind of woman that will hear "well done" from the Lord as I occupy until He comes.

Living in expectation of His return as He commands demonstrates how Christian salt and light operate effectively in a fallen world.

~

WHAT DO YOU MEAN BY THAT?

Do you prefer your meat rare, medium, or well-done? Terms are meaningless if those who use them do not agree on the definition. If I order a steak cooked to medium and it comes out bloody, it causes me to wonder what rare would look like. My definition of medium is apparently not the same as that of the restaurant kitchen. In order to communicate clearly, allow me to briefly define my views regarding Bible prophecy so we are on the same page.

First, when I talk about **prophecy** I am referring to scripture that was future when it was written. All prophetic passages regarding Christ's first coming, therefore, are prophecy; but they are now fulfilled prophecy because He came just as scripture said He would over two thousand years ago. Those prophecies are no longer in the future; they are history: He would be born in Bethlehem; His lineage would be from Jesse the father of King David; He would be born of a virgin and He would be called a Nazarene because He would be raised in Nazareth.

Spiritual Prepping for the Rapture deals only with prophecy that is still future, or **unfulfilled prophecy**. The subject is commonly referred to as that portion of the Bible dealing with the end, the end times, the latter days or the second coming of Christ. The broad term *end times*, however, can be misleading. Although the end times culminate with the physical return of Christ to the earth to establish His earthly Kingdom after the Tribulation, the end times technically began after His first coming. As I make the case for how believers in the Church Age prepare for His return, I am not placing the Church in the Tribulation when I speak of how the Church is to occupy in the end times. That would be incorrectly equating the end times with the Tribulation period alone. The Church Age began in the end times but it will end at the Rapture before the Tribulation.

Peter uses the term this way: "But the end of all things is at hand; therefore be serious and watchful in your prayers." [1 Peter 4:7] Peter is telling believers that the end is "at hand" or has arrived because Christ has come and will come again and

His return is imminent. He refers to the *end* as already in effect for the early Church; it has been the *end* for over two thousand years and the Church Age goes on. Consider Paul's words to Timothy in 2 Timothy 3:1. His discussion of the *last days [end times]* reads like our front page headlines. We are in the last days and so were Peter and Paul. But we are not yet in the Tribulation or the Kingdom.

As a child going to Sunday school in starched dresses and Mary Jane shoes, the first coming of Christ and His earthly ministry was a common topic. But I cannot recall ever hearing a lesson on His second coming, His return. If the return of Christ is not being taught in your church, the following fact will help you understand how seriously the Lord views His return: **The Lord's first coming and His second coming are both stages of one event—His coming to the earth.**

This is why both comings are prophesied in Old Testament passages with no distinction made between the two such as in Isaiah 61:2. [See also Luke 4:16-19.] The Bible refers to the end times as that period of time from the first coming to the second because it is considered one event by God. Both comings must not be separated theologically and one should not be emphasized over the other. In His first coming Christ died to redeem the earth. At His return, He will claim that which He bought with His blood and He will reign over it. It requires the full out-pouring of God's purpose in both the first and second comings of Christ to restore all things to His original intention and to give Christ Jesus the glory He deserves. If the second coming is not taught, we recognize only half of His divine purpose.

Both comings work together in spite of a gap in the completion—even though He comes, leaves for a while, and then returns. When He left at His ascension in the first chapter of Acts He sent the Comforter, the Holy Spirit, as a gift of love to His believers because His presence had been such a life-changing event. His Spirit holds His place within the believers until we are with Him again and His Spirit is with us forever [John 14:15-21]. We are *in* Christ because He is *in* us in the person of the Holy Spirit; the Church alone has the distinction of being called those who are *in Christ*, which has great distinction when we find that only those in Christ are Raptured or Resurrected at the Rapture event. [1 Thessalonians 4:14; 16]

As I speak about the Church in the end times, this does not place the Church Age in the earthly Kingdom Age. The Church Age ends with the Rapture/Resurrection of the Church before the Kingdom Age begins. Jesus corrected His own disciples when they incorrectly thought He would set up His Kingdom at His first coming: "Now as they heard these things, He spoke another parable, because He was near Jerusalem and because they thought the Kingdom of God would appear immediately. Therefore He said: 'A certain nobleman went into a far country to receive for himself a kingdom and to return.'" [Luke 19:11-12] Jesus was preparing them to wait before the Kingdom would come; to wait until He would return.

I hold a future view of the Kingdom. I believe Jesus Christ will return to establish His own Kingdom on the earth. How can there be an earthly Kingdom without a King on His earthly throne? The Church is not presently in the literal Kingdom nor are we setting it up for Christ in this age. This means I am **Premillennial regarding the return of Christ** because I believe He will return **before the thousand-year**

Millennial Kingdom to establish the Kingdom through His own power. Although the Kingdom is in its spiritual form during His public ministry as described in the Gospels [John 3:5-8], it is not literal until His second coming. Christ made this clear during His trial when He testified to Pilate "…but now My kingdom is not from here." [John 18:36]

Thirdly, I believe in a **Pretribulation Rapture/Resurrection of the Church**. In other words I believe the Church will be caught out of the earth **before the seven-year Tribulation of wrath begins**. How close the Rapture will be to the Tribulation we do not know. As I speak about the signs of the end times, I refer to particular signs of the Tribulation or general signs indicating the increasing deterioration of the world that will precede the return of Christ. The closer we are to the Tribulation, the closer we are to a Pretribulation Rapture. The Rapture itself has no specific signs; it is a sign-less event. The Church is to live by faith not by sight. [Hebrews 11:1] Because we are not to know the day or the hour, we must live in a constant state of expectation, which is the Lord's intention. However spiritual discernment about the times in which we live enables us to determine His will in the changing atmosphere of the latter days. Spiritual wisdom enables us to live already-ready while working and waiting.

The fourth point of clarification is about what is meant by the **Church**. Literally **the Church refers to the body of Christ**. [Ephesians 1:22-23] Although each true believer is an individual member, together we comprise the body—many members with different gifts but one body of Christ. [1 Corinthians 12:12-31] Therefore there is supernatural unity between Christ and believers. [John 17:20-23] We may come from buildings with different names over the door; but we are saved by grace through faith in Christ alone, not of works. Therefore when I use the word Church with a capital letter, it refers to the redeemed body of believers in Jesus Christ that come to faith during the period of time from the day of Pentecost in Acts chapter two when the Holy Spirit came to indwell believers to the day of the Rapture/Resurrection of the Church, whenever that day may be. The day of the Rapture is the day the door of the Church is closed. Grace is still present in the Tribulation and many will come to salvation but they will be Tribulation Saints, not Church Age believers.

When I refer to the church with a small *c,* it refers to systems and denominations and physical buildings for the practice of the Christian religion.

Finally, I use what is called a **dispensational method of interpreting the Bible.** In this method, God is seen as administering the affairs of this world in "various stages of revelation in the process of time." These stages are called dispensations or economies of time. Note that these dispensations have nothing to do with how people are saved; salvation is always by grace through faith in Christ alone, not of works. [Ephesians 2:8-10] However God's method of revelation differs. Following is a summary of the basic tenets of the dispensational method:

1. The Bible is interpreted in a **consistent and literal** manner. For example when the Bible says the Church, it is the Church. When the Bible says Israel, it is Israel.
2. Scripture is seen as divided by God into **time periods for the administration of the world called dispensations** [Ephesians 1:9, 10]: *Innocence,* From creation to the fall. *Conscience,* From the fall to the flood. *Human*

Government, From the flood to Abraham. *Promise,* From Abraham to Moses. *Law/Israel,* From Moses to the Church. *Grace/Church,* From the Church Age to the Second Coming of Christ and the Millennial Kingdom. *Kingdom,* From the Millennial Kingdom to the New Heavens and New Earth. [Revelation 20:1-15;21:1]

3. **Israel and the Church are different and distinct entities** in God's plan. Dispensationalists strongly deny the scriptural integrity of Replacement Theology which replaces Israel with the Church in future prophecy.

4. **The glory of God in a multifaceted way is the goal of history**. Mankind has failed every test in the administering of grace through the dispensations of time. For the most part, only a remnant is saved in any age. [Romans 11:5] The failure of man to administer world affairs displays his dependence on God and demonstrates God's glory over His own creation throughout time.

5. Prophetic scripture is yet **future,** from the Rapture of the Church to the thousand-year [Millennial] Kingdom to eternity.

[Demy, Timothy J. Ice, Thomas. *Fast Facts on Bible Prophecy from A to Z.* Eugene, Oregon: Harvest House Publishers, 1997, pp. 66-70.]

The dispensational method prevents common error in interpretation and also answers some big questions as they emerge. Following is a simple timeline of events that emerges when the Bible is interpreted literally and future.

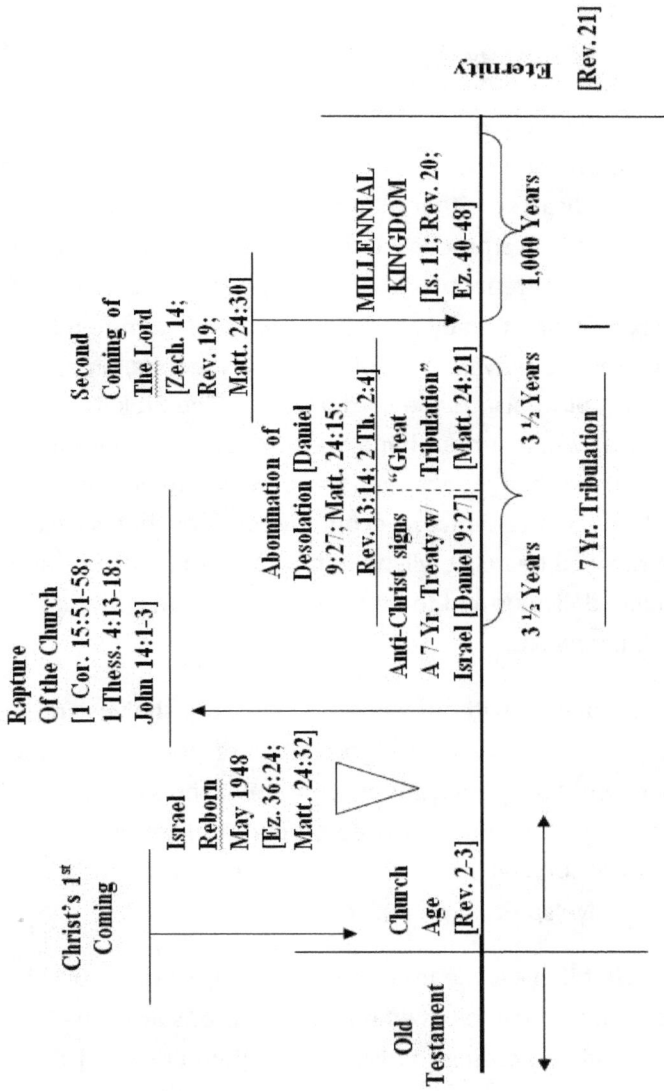

Christ's 1st Coming

Israel Reborn May 1948 [Ez. 36:24; Matt. 24:32]

Rapture Of the Church [1 Cor. 15:51-58; 1 Thess. 4:13-18; John 14:1-3]

Second Coming of The Lord [Zech. 14; Rev. 19; Matt. 24:30]

Abomination of Desolation [Daniel 9:27; Matt. 24:15; Rev. 13:14; 2 Th. 2:4]

"Great Tribulation" [Matt. 24:21]

Anti-Christ signs A 7-Yr. Treaty w/ Israel [Daniel 9:27]

Old Testament

Church Age [Rev. 2-3]

MILLENNIAL KINGDOM [Is. 11; Rev. 20; Ez. 40-48]

Eternity [Rev. 21]

3 ½ Years   3 ½ Years   1,000 Years

7 Yr. Tribulation

15

1

THE SECRET OF SURVIVAL

If you type the word "survival" into an internet search engine, you will find countless sites about how to survive during catastrophic disaster, either man-made or natural. I am not a survivalist but I am a practical Christian. How would I tell a young person to prepare for the challenges of the end times? Assuming they are already a believer, I would recommend hard work and the wise investment of the money, goods, time, talents and spiritual gifts the Lord provides. The Bible tells us to work hard at whatever our hand finds to do. Personally I am also concerned that younger generations are too dependent on pre-packaged convenience. If economy requires that we scale back to rice and beans, it will help to be able to make rice and beans taste delicious and to be able to cook them without the use of a microwave.

If money is without value and the store shelves are empty, those who survive are those who are clever enough to work with what they have and be content at the same time. However hard work and advanced preparation are not enough. The secret of survival in the case of emergency requires comprehensive spiritual preparation.

What if every means of basic survival is taken away? Can the Lord provide for us when our provisions are gone? Yes. He will provide according to His purpose. [Romans 8:28] *The* most important survival skill any believer of any time can develop is not about what to eat or what to wear or where to find shelter. The secret to survival is: *to live by faith and hope.*

I am aware this may not be the just-add-water solution you were hoping for. If living by faith involved something as simple as rubbing two rocks together, this could be a best-selling book—but it would be a fraud. True faith isn't a cheap commodity; it is the most powerful and effective weapon ever devised and it takes wisdom to master it because it is the Master who masters it in us. It is not natural; *it is supernatural*. For that reason, no one can take it from us!

To live by faith means literally to learn to *exist* by faith, to depend on Christ for life and Godliness—food, shelter, emotional health and, above all, spiritual hope. This is Practical Christianity 101! We are to *abide in Christ,* to live in Him, and He in us! [John 15:1-11] We are to pitch our tent with Christ and live the practical Christian life in spiritual victory in the days to come. The ability to live or abide in Christ more closely is the answer to every problem the Christian has.

> *"Now faith is the substance of things hoped for, the evidence of things not seen." [Hebrews 11:1]*

Faith is the substance of hope and yet both faith and hope are intangible. This is why it is difficult to "get" faith or "have" hope. How do we obtain something that has no real substance—something we cannot touch?

First, it is difficult to separate faith from hope which is why they are often spoken of together. Faith requires a focus and a motivation. How can there be faith when there is nothing to have faith "in?" But when we have a blessed hope to fix our faith upon, faith now has both a focus and a reason to have faith. Faith becomes something of real substance in our life. We begin to abide in Christ fueled by a hope of a future deliverance.

I have taught Bible prophecy for forty years. In end times prophecy, Christ provides a framework of the future on which we can build living hope in Him. He does not want us to flounder around without any discernable guidelines, ignorant about the most exciting events of history. He wants us to be motivated to work, watch and wait as He intended the Church should live.

Paul communicated this truth to the Thessalonian church when he revealed to them the mystery of the Rapture:

"But I do not want you to be ignorant, brethren, concerning those who have fallen asleep, lest you sorrow as others who have no hope...For the Lord Himself will descend from heaven with a shout, with the voice of an archangel, and with the trumpet of God. And the dead in Christ will rise first. Then we who are alive and remain shall be caught up together with them in the clouds to meet the Lord in the air. And thus we shall always be with the Lord. Therefore comfort one another with these words." [1 Thessalonians 4:13-18]

The imminent Rapture is a living hope and a constant comfort. It is a real future event on which we can fix our faith. Although the potential for global destruction is much greater now than when I was a child, I have no fear of the future. I don't have a bomb shelter in my back yard. What I have is much better and I want to share with you how to live by faith and hope in the end times. Those that are preparing for His any-moment return can live abundantly—in informed and excited anticipation, instead of fear. We can trade insecurity for a spiritually thrilling lifestyle.

PREPARE FOR WAR

As we wait in hope, it would be a great mistake to be complacent. In order to occupy until He comes, believers must spiritually train to live by faith. The believer's training is demanding; the weapons of faith are sharpened in battle. This is no video game—the stakes are real and heroes are honored. Is the Church prepared for war?

Warfare is already familiar territory for the believer. At the moment of conversion we are enlisted into battle with Satan our accuser. Satan is the ultimate terrorist with a demon army. [Ephesians 6:12] The good news is that "we are more than conquerors through Him who loved us." [Romans 8:37]

Spiritual warfare takes on a more intense dimension during the Tribulation; spiritual warfare will become a visible earth-bound reality. The remnant will be fighting demons in the guise of armies. This results when Satan and his demons are defeated by Michael the angel of Israel. Satan is thrown to the earth and no longer has access to heaven. This makes him very angry. [Revelation 12:7-12]

"Therefore rejoice, O heavens, and you who dwell in them! Woe to the inhabitants of the earth and the sea! For the devil has come down to you, having great wrath, because he knows that he has a short time." [Revelation 12:12]

I am so thankful to my Lord that He has saved me from the determined time of wrath to come. However, we will still fight battles in the transition time before the Tribulation. The Spirit of Lawlessness [2 Thessalonians 2:7] is already operating. We need to keep our weapons sharp and at the ready for the daily battle. "But know this, that in the last days perilous times

19

will come…" [2 Timothy 3:1]. We are to be constantly on guard because Satan is like a prowling lion, seeking someone to devour. [1 Peter 5:8]

How intense our warfare becomes before we are caught out in the Rapture is in the Lord's control. We would do well to familiarize ourselves with what is coming in order to stand against the advance guard. For the most part, global change is gradual in order to deceive the world into apathy; but the conspiracy of evil is already at work. Ignoring Christ's advance warnings and battle plans would be like a general who marches into the front lines without scouting the enemy. Just as residents of California say *the big one is coming,* referring to a great earthquake, so the big and final global conflict is coming with all the accompanying signs before it.

As a preview of coming attractions, our Lord described how the battle will intensify to terrible proportions in the Tribulation: "For then there will be great tribulation, such as has not been since the beginning of the world until this time, no, nor ever shall be. And unless those days were shortened, no flesh would be saved; but for the elect's sake those days will be shortened." [Matthew 24:21-22] If the tribulation is the worst time on the face of the earth that means it will be worse than the persecution of Christians during the Roman Empire, worse than the Bubonic plague, worse than World Wars I and II and even the holocaust. We can only speculate that the transition leading up to the Tribulation will be a very demanding time for the Church even though we are raptured before the actual Tribulation period begins.

THE GOOD NEWS

Talk of Armageddon doesn't make me nervous but it did when I was an uninformed, naïve young Christian. The worst mistake I could have made when I heard about literal prophecy would have been to dismiss it as too frightening, too hard, or too confusing. When the subject of prophecy comes up, the reaction is usually fear, scoffing, apathy, or excitement about the topic. Don't let a fear of the future keep you from studying it; the truth vanquishes fear. For those who ridicule prophecy, I pray the Holy Spirit will open their hearts in His time.

One point may help with the fear issue. The word Armageddon, which is the final battle of the Tribulation, has been wrongly associated with the end of the world. Dear friends, the Bible teaches that the battle isn't the end of the world—it is just the beginning. Christ returns to defeat His enemies, rescue the Tribulation remnant from annihilation, and then establish His glorious earthly Kingdom. [Zechariah 14] During His great and glorious reign of a thousand years, the believing remnants of all ages will be with Him [Revelation 20:4-6], including the remnant of believers known as the Church. The Millennial Kingdom then transitions into the eternal Kingdom called the new heaven and new earth. [Revelation 21:1] We will live with Him forever in New Jerusalem, a glorious city beyond description. All things will become new, pure and eternally secure. It will be beyond wonderful. The best is yet to come. We have an incredible future to look forward to.

BEWARE DOCTRINS OF FALSE PEACE

Great lessons to aid us in the present are also learned from the past. [1 Corinthians 10:6] The nation of Judah prior to the Babylonian Captivity believed they were secure because the Lord was with them. But because of their idolatry, the prophet

Jeremiah was instructed to warn Judah that destruction was coming. False priests and prophets told the people what they wanted to hear; they refused to believe that God would allow His people to go into captivity and persecuted Jeremiah for daring to speak the truth.

Jeremiah 8:4, 11—"Moreover you shall say to them, 'Thus says the LORD...they have healed the hurt of the daughter of My people slightly, saying, 'Peace, peace!' when there is no peace."

A situation with startling similarity exists today. Many, even in the Church, do not believe that the Lord would allow America to fall. They cry "peace, peace" when there is no peace. For example a segment of churches believe Christianity will successfully evangelize the world before Christ returns making it "Christian." They believe Christ established His earthly Kingdom at His first coming and the Church merely needs to complete its global expanse. In order to support their flawed view, they lift Biblical passages such as Micah 4:3 out of context: "They shall beat their swords into plowshares, and their spears into pruning hooks; nation shall not lift up sword against nation, neither shall they learn war anymore."

Ironically this passage is carved into the United Nations building in New York City like a boast. It should be an indictment against the UN for failing miserably in their quest to bring peace to the world as they promised. Good intentions don't count.

The Church will also fail to bring about world peace just as the United Nations has failed. Since the turn of the last century, massive efforts at world evangelism have failed to convert enough people to divert a hell bent world. Many are called but few are chosen. [Ephesians 2:8-10; Acts 13:48]

22

Christians are being deceived by man's utopian dream of peace through his own efforts and outside of God's plan of the ages.

Look again at the Micah 4:3 passage. If taken in the context of the book of Micah, the passage is not about global evangelization by a victorious Church; it describes the Lord's reign in Zion [Israel] after He returns at the end of the Tribulation. Only when the Prince of Peace returns will peace reign on the earth, not because the UN or the Church accomplishes it but because Christ rules with a strong authoritarian hand after His wrath has been poured out. When Micah 4:3 is taken out of context, it can be made to say the opposite of God's intention. Those who claim we are in the age of peace and can put our weapons away are at the wrong end of His divine timeline.

Those who interpret prophecy literally quote Joel 3:10-11 as the event that is on the horizon. "Beat your plowshares into swords and your pruning hooks into spears; let the weak say, 'I am strong.'" Assemble and come all you nations, and gather together all around. Cause Your mighty ones to go down there, O LORD." Joel speaks of war, not peace, when the armies of the world gather at the close of the Tribulation for the final battle of Armageddon. The book of Joel prophesies that war comes *before* the kingdom because Christ must first return and be victorious against His enemies before He establishes lasting peace.

The return of Christ before the Kingdom is known as the Premillennial return of Christ. This is the correct interpretation when scripture is taken literally and future. Only the Premillennial return of Christ ensures that God receives all the glory, not the church. The world is perched on the brink of global war, not true peace. Is the Church preparing for peace when they should be preparing for coming war? If so they are vulnerable and unprepared, like sitting ducks for deception.

1 Thessalonians 5:3-11—"For when they say, 'Peace and safety!' then sudden destruction comes upon them, as labor pains upon a pregnant woman. And they shall not escape. But you, brethren, are not in darkness, so that this Day should overtake you as a thief. You are all sons of light and sons of the day. We are not of the night nor of darkness. Therefore let us not sleep, as others do, but let us watch and be sober. For those who sleep, sleep at night, and those who get drunk are drunk at night. But let us who are of the day be sober, putting on the breastplate of faith and love, and as a helmet the hope of salvation. For God did not appoint us to wrath, but to obtain salvation through our Lord Jesus Christ, who died for us, that whether we wake or sleep, we should live together with Him. Therefore comfort each other and edify one another, just as you also are doing. "

If the Church is preparing for peace, it is a false peace. When the battle intensifies, they will be deceived and caught off guard. We are to prepare for war, putting on our spiritual armor to hold our ground for Christ until He comes. Determine to be sons of light and train for war. Being prepared is half the battle.

~

Practical Prepping - A Cottage Business

The Cottage Business I began in my home was the seed of an idea that eventually led to a full-time business for our family. In addition to culinary herbs which I used in our restaurant and now in my home, I grew everlasting herbs and flowers which I harvested for dried wreaths and decorations. These everlasting accents were one of the best sellers in our retail business. Now I make them for home, for gifts, and occasionally for sale in a friend's tea room.

The following are the everlastings I grow or glean from the meadows: goldenrod, sour dock, grasses, yellow and white yarrow, sea lavender, German statice, baby's breath, astilbe, roses, peonies, hydrangea, pine cones, rose hips, dried crabapples, Lady's Mantle, bittersweet, wormwood, Sweet Annie, Artemisia's, tansy, hops, celosia, globe amaranth, larkspur, bay leaf, blooming thyme and blooming spearmint, dried sage and bay leaf.

Dried flowers were used to decorate early American homes during the winter. Even a plentiful bouquet of dried grasses and flowers tied with twine is charming when displayed as a welcoming swag on a front door. Fill baskets with flowers and dried berries for an autumn table centerpiece. Dried wreaths preserve the garden's summer bloom and cost little.

A true everlasting flower is one that holds its shape and color when hung and air dried. By September the rafters of my country kitchen are filled with bunches of drying herbs and flowers. Slowly I add to the harvest as each variety comes into bloom. By autumn I have enough bounty to begin attaching dried bunches to straw wreaths with greening pins. I use a hot glue gun to add fragile blooms to the full wreath. Berries such as dried crabapples, bittersweet and rose hips add seasonal touches. When displayed indoors out of full light and humidity, everlasting wreaths can last for years.

~

2

THE RAPTURE/RESURRECTION OF THE CHURCH—

OUR BLESSED HOPE

Have you ever felt hopeless? Without hope, no one can survive but the believer is never without it because in Christ we have the sure hope of eternal life. As a down payment of that promise, He gave us the gift of the indwelling Holy Spirit. [John 14] The Holy Spirit is the engagement ring signifying our betrothal to Jesus Christ. But the Church Age believer has more. We have an imminent hope.

We are to be "looking for the blessed hope and glorious appearing of our great God and Savior Jesus Christ…" This blessed hope is imminent because it can happen at any moment. [Titus 2:13] The believing remnant of the Church Age is waiting for the first stage of this appearing, the Rapture of the Church, when Christ will suddenly appear in the clouds and in less than it takes to blink an eye He will catch His bride away. I cannot imagine a more exciting prospect to hope for. Instantaneously we shall go from a world of grief and death to eternal abundant life!

Our hope in His return is even more than escape from this fallen world; it is going home to be with Him. "And thus we shall always be with the Lord. Therefore comfort one another with these words." [1 Thessalonians 4:17-18] If it is His will that we die before the Rapture that is also our deliverance to Him. In either case, either in physical death or Rapture [translation of the body], the Church will be taken before the Tribulation and spend eternity with Christ.

Brides spend a great deal of time planning their wedding day. Recently we were invited to a charming garden wedding where the beautiful bride arrived riding a majestic horse with a mantle of flowers around his neck. Her father lifted her from the saddle and then walked her down the aisle to her dumbstruck groom. It was the most touching bridal entrance I have yet to see. However the entrance of Christ for His bride will surpass any celebration we could humanly conceive.

The Rapture will be spectacular not just for the splendor of His appearing. His coming will be announced with a shout of an archangel and with the trumpet call of God the Father. That audible declaration will pierce our hearts and thrill us beyond description. At the Rapture only those in Christ will hear this divine announcement; only those taken will see Him. He does not descend completely to the earth at the Rapture, only to the atmosphere where the clouds hide Him. The ceremony is a private event for the invited only. The lost world will wonder where the Christians have gone, leaving the chaos from their disappearance and earthly commitments behind them. The truth is that the bride has gone home.

Although it will be our spiritual wedding day whether we are alive or awaiting resurrection, Christ has staged the Rapture as representative of all the precious promises we receive through salvation in Jesus Christ. Even more significant, the event is for His glory.

VICTORY OVER DEATH

The Rapture is the blessed hope because it is a statement of Christ's ultimate victory over death itself; the benefits are ours in Christ. 1 Corinthians 15:26—"The last enemy that will be destroyed is death." "Death is swallowed up in victory." "O Death, where is your sting? O Hades, where is your victory?" [1 Corinthians 15:54-55] As Jesus told Martha, "I am the resurrection and the life. He who believes in Me, though he may die, he shall live. And whoever lives and believes in Me shall never die. Do you believe this?" [John 11:25-26] To punctuate this truth, He raised her brother Lazarus from the dead as a preview of His own resurrection.

Belief in His resurrection is essential to salvation because "if Christ is not risen, then our preaching is empty and your faith is also empty." [1 Corinthians 15:14] We worship a living God and because He lives, we shall live with Him in eternity. [John 14:19] The Rapture event is a graphic demonstration of this truth.

The Rapture is our Lord's definitive statement of His power over sin which leads to death. "I am He who lives, and was dead, and behold, I am alive forevermore. Amen. And I have the keys of Hades and of Death." [Revelation 1:18] Only Christ controls life and death and heaven and hell. The Rapture/Resurrection of the Church is literal proof. We are the fortunate participants. [Romans 6:4]

PRESENT WITH THE LORD

The Rapture is the blessed hope because believers long to be with Him, to see Him in His glory and to abide with Him forever. From the day He ascended to the Father, the redeemed have waited for His return. The night He was betrayed, Christ announced His departure to His close disciples and comforted them with these words:

John 14:1-3 – "Let not your heart be troubled; you believe in God, believe also in Me. In My Father's house are many mansions; if it were not so, I would have told you. I go to prepare a place for you. And if I go and prepare a place for you, I will come again and receive you to Myself; that where I am there you may be also."

Paul shared with the Philippian church that he was hard-pressed to decide what he wanted most: to live longer for Christ in this life or to die so that he could depart and be with Christ in heaven. He admitted that departing and being with His Lord is far better but the decision was not his to make; Paul's life, like ours, is in the Lord's hands. Someday, perhaps in the very near future, He will call us home. That is a very blessed hope.

THE WEDDING OF THE LAMB AND GLORIFICATION OF THE BRIDE

The Rapture of the Church is our blessed hope because it is the wedding of the Lamb and the presenting of the bride. The ceremony begins in heaven after the Rapture but the feast will continue into the Millennial Kingdom on earth. At the Second Coming event, the physical return of Christ to the earth, He returns at least seven years after the Rapture; by this time the bride is now the wife of Christ and returns with Him.

Revelation 19:6b-9--"*'Alleluia! For the Lord God Omnipotent reigns! Let us be glad and rejoice and give Him glory, for the marriage of the Lamb has come, and His wife has made herself ready.' And to her it was granted to be arrayed in fine linen, clean and bright, for the fine linen is the righteous acts of the saints. Then he said to me, 'Write: "Blessed are those who are called to the marriage supper of the Lamb!"'*

Our wedding gown will be the robe of righteousness given to us through the blood of Jesus Christ. The adornment of the gown is the gold, silver and precious stones symbolizing the work done for Christ as we waited for His return. The reward ceremony where we receive our "well done" by Christ called the Bema is discussed in a later chapter. Work has nothing to do with our salvation but it is evidence of our devotion to Christ.

The gilding of the gown that makes the bride radiant is the glory we share in Him. The Rapture is that momentous event in which the golden chain of sanctification through the Holy Spirit for the believer is completed with the final stage— the glorification: "Moreover whom He predestined, these He also called; whom He called, these He also justified; and whom He justified, these He also glorified." [Romans 8:29-30] The Rapture/Resurrection is the day of our glorification in Christ! The process by which the Spirit conforms us to the image of the Son is finally finished. Personally I long for the day I can stand before my Lord knowing this work in progress called Sharon is complete. Come, Lord Jesus!

ONE WITH CHRIST

The Rapture of the Church is also our blessed hope because we become one with Christ in spiritual union. I am sure and certain that I cannot begin to imagine what it will be like to be one with Christ in eternity. My limited humanity doesn't equip me with that level of imagination. I am also humbled to know that the Bible plainly teaches He wants to be one with me.

Before His death, Jesus told the disciples, "A little while longer and the world will see Me no more, but you will see Me. Because I live, you will live also. At that day you will know that I am in My Father, and you in Me, and I in you." "If anyone loves

Me, he will keep My word; and My Father will love him, and We will come to him and make Our home with him." [John 14:19-20, 23] On earth this was previewed by the indwelling Holy Spirit. [John 14:15-16] But in heaven it will be a higher dimension.

At the Rapture/Resurrection, the remnant of true believers are actually a unique gift from the Father to the Son for eternity. Christ prayed for us, this remnant, the night before He died for our sins: "Holy Father, keep through Your name those whom You have given Me, that they may be one as We are. While I was with them in the world, I kept them in Your name. Those whom You gave Me I have kept; and none of them is lost except the son of perdition, that the Scripture might be fulfilled." [John 17:11b-12] The son of perdition or the son of hell was Judas who betrayed Him. He alone was lost because it was ordained by God in eternity past.

Throughout John 17, Christ speaks of His strong desire that the Church not only find unity among the members of the remnant but unity with the Father and Son. Then He looks longingly toward the future: "Father, I desire that they also whom You gave Me may be with Me where I am, that they may behold My glory which You have given Me; for you loved Me before the foundation of the world." [John 17:24] The Rapture is that moment in which we behold His glory in heaven; it is also the moment when the Church is glorified in Him! Oh what a day that will be!

THE RAPTURE/RESURRECTION OF THE CHURCH

The Rapture is a new concept to many in Amillennial [no millennium] denominations that do not teach a literal prophetic fulfillment. I attended such a denomination for over twenty years but I now know that the Bible speaks clearly of the Rapture and that my generation could be the one to see the return of Christ for the Church. To be clear, Christ's return has been imminent from the time He left. [Acts 1:9-11] For over two thousand years it *could* have happened at any moment, which is why it is called an imminent or any-moment event. There is nothing in scripture that must happen before Christ returns to receive His Church in the clouds. Believers do not look for signs of the Rapture; there aren't any. Instead, we speculate on signs that point to the beginning of the Tribulation. If the Tribulation is near, the Rapture is nearer.

What a fantastic moment to anticipate! Paul joyously said "We shall not all sleep, but we shall all be changed..." [1 Corinthians 15:51] Imagine a remnant of believers who will never experience physical death before they see Christ.

His return is in two stages. At the Rapture return, which is the first stage, the living are translated or changed without experiencing physical death. Paul states that this happens so quickly it cannot be detected by the naked eye. It is also the time of the resurrection of the dead in Christ—in fact those whose bodies are "sleeping" are re-united with their soul/spirits before the living are translated. He returns to "receive" the resurrected and translated [raptured] believers of the Church Age in the air of the earth's atmosphere. [John 14:1-3] We go up to meet Him in the clouds but His feet do not touch the earth in this stage. [1 Thessalonians 4:17] Only those raptured or resurrected will see Him. To the rest of the world, it will be as if a segment of the population has simply disappeared.

Make no mistake—the enemies of God already have explanations for where we will have gone and are ready to spin the truth. They will not say we are with God in heaven. They will lie to further their own agenda. Corrupt leaders may even take credit for our disappearance, claiming they are ridding the world of negative influence that is preventing the quantum leap in man's spiritual evolution. This bizarre explanation is already held by many in the New Age movement. Grand church officials who are false teachers will claim the true believers were left behind and it is the evil fomenters of strife that have been taken out...all those religious terrorists...and good riddance. These lies will comfort those who were left; they will want to believe the lie. [2 Thessalonians 2]

The second stage of His return is His dramatic entrance to the earth's surface at the end of the Tribulation. This stage is more commonly referred to as The Second Coming [Matthew 24:27-30; Acts 1:9-11; Zechariah 14; Revelation 19:11-21] or the climax of the Day of the Lord.

At this time His feet will land on the exact spot from which He ascended [Acts 1]. He will return physically, coming down from the atmospheric clouds and landing on The Mount of Olives in Jerusalem. Unlike the Rapture, at this time He returns at the end of the Tribulation in great glory; and He will be seen by the entire world. Revelation 1:7 states "every eye will see Him..." Only in this day of modern technology could Christ be seen within the context of humanity by every eye. That is now possible through satellite communication.

Christ has been waiting to return to the earth for over two thousand years and His entrance will be worthy of His divinity. His appearance to Jerusalem will be spectacular, a triumphal entry fit for the King of the universe with all the pomp and circumstance and divine glory that He deserves. No poor stable and humble trough awaits Him this time. He returns on a white war horse clothed in indescribable majesty. The honor of His divinity is displayed in many crowns and He wears His titles as a victory banner. We follow in His entourage wearing the white robes of His righteousness on white horses. His glory will shake the cosmos with the power of His radiance. [Revelation 19:11-16; Matthew 24:29-30]

Zechariah 14:4—"And in that day His feet will stand on the Mount of Olives, which faces Jerusalem on the east."

Matthew 24:29-30—"Immediately after the tribulation of those days the sun will be darkened, and the moon will not give its light; the stars will fall from heaven, and the powers of the heavens will be shaken. Then the sign of the Son of Man will appear in heaven, and then all the tribes of the earth will mourn, and they will see the Son of Man coming on the clouds of heaven with power and great glory."

Like the old black and white westerns my brothers and I watched on Saturday mornings, the cavalry always arrived just in time to save the settlers. So Christ will return at the moment when Jerusalem seems lost; He will pull them like a smoking brand from the fire and will annihilate their attackers. *[Zechariah 14:12-13]*

Hollywood could not write this. They could not do justice to our God, awesome and terrible in battle. The Lord's enemies disintegrate before His eyes at the Word of His mouth. He is our conquering king, fearsome in battle but mighty to save. In that day His robes will be stained with the blood of His enemies. Isaiah 63:4—"For the day of vengeance is in My heart, and the year of My redeemed has come."

I detailed both stages of His coming to contrast the two and yet show the importance of both. How can God be sufficiently glorified if any stage of Christ's return is passed over by those who think prophesy is too controversial? Ignoring prophecy or interpreting it wrongly omits a large segment of God's Word—large sections of the major and minor prophets as well as the entire book of The Revelation. Editing the Word of God has severe consequences as the Bible makes abundantly clear. [Revelation 22:18-19] A curse is called down on those who edit the Bible by refusing to teach prophecy. But the curse also falls on those who neglect reading it for themselves. All Scripture is inspired by God and is "profitable" as Paul said to Timothy. Scripture is available to equip the believer [2 Timothy 3:16-17]; and prophecy, especially, prepares each generation with a forecast of future events. Why would we not take full advantage of such a resource?

The Bible is the complete story of the Lord cover to cover; every passage has been inspired by the Holy Spirit for a purpose and every passage deserves to be taught. When I first heard teaching on future prophecy, I began to understand how God's sovereign hand directs all things toward a divine climax.

Ephesians 1:10—"...having made known to us the mystery of His will, according to His good pleasure which He purposed in Himself, that in the dispensation of the fullness of the times He might gather together in one all things in Christ, both which are in heaven and which are on earth—in Him."

The Lord is bringing *all* things in the universe together in Christ to resolve all outstanding covenants and promises and it takes two returns to complete His purpose. I can think of no better happy ending.

HOPE UPON HOPE

The Bible reveals strong evidence for the Rapture/Resurrection of the Church *before* the Seven-Year Tribulation begins. [Rapture/Resurrection Event: 1 Thessalonians 4:13-18; 1 Corinthians 15:51-58; John 14:1-3] At the moment of the Rapture, the living remnant will be changed or translated into bodies suited to eternal life. The souls and spirits of those who died in Christ prior to the Rapture will return with Him and be united with their resurrected bodies which will also be made eternity-ready. Notice that the Rapture is only for those "in Christ." [1 Thessalonians 4:16] They are Church Age believers who have the indwelling Holy Spirit. We are "in Christ" because He is in us in the person of the Holy Spirit [John 14].

The Holy Spirit came to the Church on the Day of Pentecost, Acts 2. Therefore, the Church Age consists of those believers from Pentecost to the day of the Rapture [John 14:16-17]. The Old Testament Saints and Tribulation Saints are resurrected at the close of the Tribulation in order to enter into the blessings of the Kingdom age and receive the covenant promises. [Revelation 20:4-6; Daniel 12:1-2]

The scriptural evidence for a Pretribulation Rapture is presented in the next chapter. Clearly, those who will be taken out before the Tribulation begins have a unique perspective. Our hope affects the way in which we occupy until Christ returns for us. [Luke 19:13]

IT'S NOT OUR WAR

The Church does not have to feel guilty that we will not endure the Tribulation; the Rapture is our blessed hope. We do not take pleasure in the fact that those who remain after the Rapture will go through the Tribulation. We are spared because the Church is redeemed by Christ, not because of our own merit. It is not our war because it is not our call and it is not for our honor; it is for His. We are His special gift from the Father; why would He toss His gift in the fire.

Some truly believe we do not deserve to be taken home before wrath falls on men. They are right; we do not deserve it. Thank God Christ's blood has us covered. The Age of Grace is the time of the Church—for His glory; the time of wrath is to display His glory in claiming His Kingdom and restoring Israel. [Daniel 9:24—Only seven years of this determined time for Israel remains—the Tribulation. But Israel will be saved out of it. Jeremiah 31:31ff; 30:7; Zechariah 13:9]

APATHY AND APOSTACY

Although we are not appointed to wrath there is a danger that those who will not go through the Tribulation become complacent. The Church as a whole has become so apathetic about the future of God's plan that many are unprepared for what may come before the Rapture takes us home. This complacency is even more prevalent for those who wrongly believe things will get better, not worse. They are among the scoffers of the end times [2 Peter 3:3].

If Christ's return is near we will see continued social and political change on a global scale. It must be so for the fulfillment of prophecy. Antichrist's demonic kingdom will eventually be global in power. It is described as a one-world government, one-world economy, and one-world false religious system. [See Revelation 13, 17 and 18; Daniel 7:19-28.]

America no longer holds the undisputed title of the world's last super power. Have you noticed how rarely the term "super power" is applied to the US in recent years? Our nation must lose a great deal more of its status and economic stability in order to submit our national sovereignty willingly to the global government of Antichrist during the Tribulation [Revelation 13; 17]. Will America fall due to economic collapse? Internal moral collapse? Civil unrest? Invasion? Natural disaster? Man-made disaster such as an Electro Magnetic Pulse or cyber-attack? Are we ready for any contingency? Corporations have contingency plans for nearly every eventuality—does the Church? How can we work for His glory if we are not prepared for battle field conditions?

Pandemic deception is especially disturbing in these days because it infects like mass insanity. False religion promotes a kind of emotional hysteria, apostasy and delusion [Matthew 24:4-5; 2 Thessalonians 2:9-11; 1 Timothy 4:1-5; 2 Timothy 3:1-9; 4:3-5]. Truth is cleverly spun into lies [Isaiah 5:20]; and those who believe in absolute truth are ridiculed, mocked and persecuted. The postmodern culture does not believe in absolute truth and considers those who do to be intolerant of other "truths." If there is more than one truth, than the concept of truth is negated. By definition, truth is a solitary construct.

The post-modern delusion that truth is however we perceive it to be has resulted in the emotional tolerance of sin. When did loving the sinner while hating the sin become loving the sinner and tolerating the sin? A politically-correct attitude is actually considered more socially righteous than affirming absolute truth, even by many who call themselves evangelical. But the one truth, Jesus Christ, is the bedrock of our Christian faith—He is *the* way, *the* truth, and *the* life [John 14:6]. Believers cannot compromise this core belief. Without it, there is only chaos.

In addition to cultural and political chaos, natural disasters are on the increase. Earthquakes are an interesting phenomenon to track. They are indeed increasing in frequency and intensity in various or random places [Matthew 24:7]. On April 18, 2008, I awoke from a sound sleep to what I first thought was a knocking at the front door but realized our whole house was vibrating. I wondered if the Blue Angels were flying overhead but there was no sound of jet planes. It was an earthquake. An earthquake is a rare event for Central Illinois but that may not be the case in the future.

Natural disasters are not only increasing; they are breaking records for intensity. In the last ten years we have had so much wind and tornado damage in our state, the insurance companies were allowed to dramatically increase home insurance deductibles. Because we made four claims for roof damage in the last ten years, our deductible recently increased ten times the original amount.

CLUELESS OR WISE

It comes down to this—are we clueless or wise concerning the end times? The day is fast approaching when there is no in-between—that pleasant place where we can exist in blissful ignorance of the times in which we live and just go about our own business. Such clueless ones are exactly how the Lord described the lost prior to the flood in Matthew 24:37-39—"But as the days of Noah were, so also will the coming of the Son of Man be. For as in the days before the flood, they were eating and drinking, marrying and giving in marriage, until the day that Noah entered the ark, and did not know until the flood came and took them all away, so also will the coming of the Son of Man be."

They did not know until the flood came and took them all away… Did not know what? They did not know that judgment was coming. They were clueless, going about their normal, everyday life, marrying and eating and living. A complacent attitude will be judged; only this time it will be with fire, not water.

The alternative to being clueless is being wise. "Go your way, Daniel, for the words are closed up and sealed till the time of the end. Many shall be purified, made white, and refined, but the wicked shall do wickedly; and none of the wicked shall understand, but 'the wise shall understand.'" [Daniel 12:9-10] God's prophetic timeline is available to any who wish to read it, yet few take advantage of this knowledge to make them wise.

This wisdom is not of us; it begins with a healthy fear of the LORD. "The fear of the LORD is the beginning of knowledge, but fools despise wisdom and instruction." [Proverbs 1:7] The believing remnant of the end times will first and foremost be wise in the knowledge of the Lord and His Word.

Earlier in Daniel's twelfth chapter, the man of God is also given a sketch of the end times—the time in which the fullness of prophecy would be revealed. I find this verse to be one of the most revealing sound bites in the Word and it is the verse that predicts pandemic chaos: "But you, Daniel, shut up the words, and seal the book until the time of the end; many shall run to and fro, and knowledge shall increase." [Daniel 12:4]

What does it mean that many shall run to and fro and knowledge shall increase? It is obviously very significant because Daniel was told to lock it up until this condition exists. It must have great significance for the last days.

Commentators have slightly differing views on the interpretation of the passage but it comes down to this: there will be technological chaos in the end times. People will be running around like chickens with their heads cut off, as my grandfather would say, in a frenzy from the exponential increase in travel and technology and everything that results from it. Technological advances are introduced one on top of another; we scarcely adapt before the newest improvement is thrust upon us. We have become slaves to our own innovation.

More technological and scientific advances and discoveries have been made in the last one hundred years than all the ages of time that came before. We are flooded and inundated by them. The subjugation of the world by machine is no longer science fiction—it is fact. Allowing ourselves to become dependent on man-made technology has made us subservient to it. We are vulnerable to any threat that controls our technology or the power source that runs it.

That threat, that man, will ultimately be Antichrist. No man will be able to buy or sell unless they have taken his mark, 666 [Revelation 13].

The good news is that Armageddon is not our war. The Church is occupied in our own ongoing battle to hold our position for Christ. The antidote to the coming spiritual and technological chaos is to become wise in the Word and put our trust completely in the Lord [Proverbs 3:5]. We have our marching orders. His direction cuts through the chaos and shines a bright light on the paths we are to take.

~

Practical Prepping

More Than a Crumb of Daily Bread

Natural vinegar is a healthy probiotic. I take a tablespoon of vinegar that contains the "mother," the natural yeast, in my orange juice every morning. It is excellent not only as a probiotic but vinegar restores the natural PH of the system and aids digestion. Vinegar was used for acid reflux before over-the-counter drugs became popular.

Just as certain vitamin and mineral supplements are a good way to start the day, I take a healthy dose of Bible reading and prayer each morning. It sets my head in the right direction and gives the Lord first place. I used to think I didn't have time to have morning Bible study and prayer; I found out the hard way that I don't have time not to. My Bible even goes on vacation with me. Taking in His Word is like eating; if we fast from it, we begin to starve spiritually. He is not called "the bread of life" for nothing.

~

3

THE PRETRIBULATION RAPTURE

It is obvious that we need a firm grasp on faith and hope in Christ in these days—and we have it. I believe scripture strongly supports rapture before the Tribulation which is why it is a blessed hope [Titus 2:13]. The time line map is repeated on the following page to illustrate the Pretribulation Rapture as it relates to end time events. Although I believe the catching out of the Church before the Tribulation is the only interpretation that affirms God's perfect order and cuts cleanly the distinction between the Church and Israel, there are differing views on the timing. The following points will clarify the Pretribulation position.

HIS RETURN IN RELATION TO THE KINGDOM

Believers first recognize that the Second Coming of Christ physically to the earth occurs before the thousand-year Millennial Kingdom. His return before true peace in the Millennial Kingdom is called the Premillennial return of Christ. It is essential that believers recognize that Christ will return *before* His kingdom in order to establish it Himself [Revelation 19 and 20]. The Church does not accomplish it for Him. He will reign on the Throne of David from a Millennial temple He builds Himself [Zechariah 6:12-13]. The timing of the Rapture is secondary to a Premillennial doctrine. Those who believe Christ will not return until after the Kingdom are Postmillennial.

~

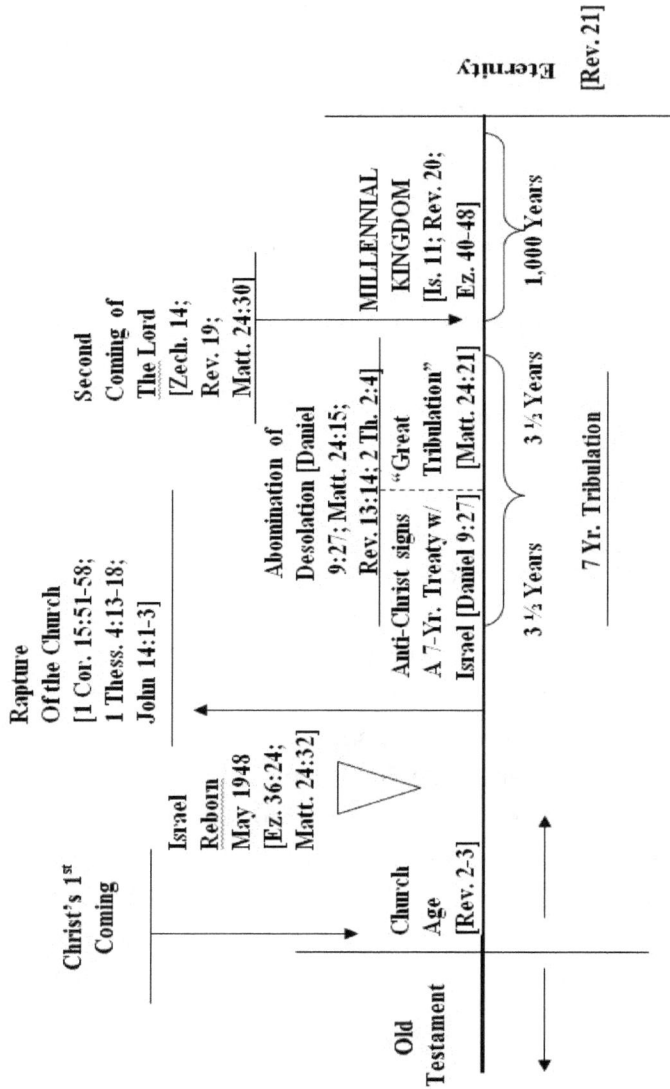

Old Testament

Christ's 1st Coming

Israel Reborn May 1948 [Ez. 36:24; Matt. 24:32]

Church Age [Rev. 2-3]

Rapture Of the Church [1 Cor. 15:51-58; 1 Thess. 4:13-18; John 14:1-3]

Abomination of Desolation [Daniel 9:27; Matt. 24:15; Rev. 13:14; 2 Th. 2:4]

Anti-Christ signs A 7-Yr. Treaty w/ Israel [Daniel 9:27]

"Great Tribulation" [Matt. 24:21]

Second Coming of The Lord [Zech. 14; Rev. 19; Matt. 24:30]

MILLENNIAL KINGDOM [Is. 11; Rev. 20; Ez. 40-48]

Eternity [Rev. 21]

3 ½ Years

3 ½ Years

7 Yr. Tribulation

1,000 Years

44

HIS RETURN IN RELATION TO THE TRIBULATION

I teach the Pretribulation Rapture view because of the evidence of scripture. The Church's presence is not required or necessary during the Tribulation. We have another purpose in God's plan and it doesn't include experiencing the most terrible period of God's unleashed wrath the world has ever known. [Matthew 24:21] The Church is The Bride of Christ [Ephesians 5:25-27, 32; John 3:29; Revelation 22:17]. The Church is saved by the blood of our Savior. In place of the filthy rags of sin we wear a spotless white wedding gown spun of His righteousness. The Bride waits in anticipation for the marriage of the Lamb [Revelation 19:7], not the Tribulation.

Why would Christ subject the Bride to seven years of divine wrath when Church Age believers are already washed in His blood? Was Christ's atonement not sufficient? Does the Church need to perform some penance beyond believing in God's grace alone through faith alone? [Ephesians 2:8-10] Is there something we must do regarding the Gospel that the two witnesses and the one hundred forty-four thousand hand-picked and sealed Jews cannot do? [Revelation 11; 7] The answer to all is "no."

Although the desire to suffer for Christ in the Tribulation and to save the lost may be the sincere desire of some in the Church, it is not God's plan that the Church should be His vehicle; that role will be restored to Israel [Romans 11]. As the ultimate warning before final judgment, a special angel envoy will be sent from the throne room of heaven from God Himself to dispense a global proclamation of the Gospel to the entire earth during the Tribulation:

Revelation 14:6-7—"Then I saw another angel flying in the midst of heaven, having the everlasting gospel to preach to those who dwell on the earth—to every nation, tribe, tongue, and people—saying with a loud voice, 'Fear God and give glory to Him, for the hour of His judgment has come; and worship Him who made heaven and earth, the sea and springs of water.'"

This is the only place in scripture to declare that the Gospel has been taken to every person on the face of the earth and it is accomplished by Christ in the Tribulation. The mandate of global evangelism as a finished work is wrongly attached to the Church.

The seven years of determined wrath are meant to punish a Christ-rejecting world [Isaiah 2:11-18] and to bring Israel into the New Covenant [Jeremiah 31:31-34; Ezekiel 36:24-28]. As Paul said in Romans 11, blindness has been allowed to happen to Israel until the full number of Gentiles or non-Jews are saved. But then the remnant of the Jews will be saved out of the purging fire of the Tribulation. [Zechariah 12:10-Zechariah 13]

But for the bride "There is therefore now no condemnation to those who are in Christ Jesus, who do not walk according to the flesh, but according to the Spirit." [Romans 8:1] No condemnation means no judgment. Our judgment was taken by Christ at the cross; it is finished for the Church. To insist those in Christ endure the determined wrath of the Tribulation degrades the definitive plan of God.

OTHER RAPTURE VIEWS

In addition to the Pretribulation Rapture, there is a view that the Church goes through the first half of the Tribulation.

46

This view is commonly called the Prewrath Rapture. Another view is the Posttribulation Rapture which holds that the Church will go through the entire seven-year Tribulation. If the Rapture were to take place during the Tribulation or after the Tribulation, it would destroy the imminent, any-moment characteristics of the event. We are told to watch and wait because we cannot know the day or hour of His coming; it is a sign-less event. [Matthew 24:36] However there are many signs for the Tribulation and for the Second Coming. The Rapture cannot be imminent if it occurs when the Tribulation has begun. We are instructed to wait for Christ's return not for the appearing of Antichrist or the unleashing of the Seals, Trumpets and Bowl judgments.

The Church is to live by faith not sight. [Hebrews 11:1] We are to live already-ready. From the time of Christ's ascension to the present day, believers are to watch and wait because the Rapture is an imminent, any-moment event. Nothing must happen before Christ returns in the clouds for the Church. General signs may indicate we are closer than ever before, but we cannot know the day. So it is that we keep watch on trends pointing to the Tribulation. If the Tribulation is drawing near, the Rapture is nearer still.

The Posttribulation Rapture is the easiest to discredit. Consider this. After the Lord's return, He gathers all the saved who survive the Tribulation into His Kingdom [Matthew 24:31]. Only believers are allowed into the Kingdom; they are the wheat separated from the weeds or tares [Matthew 24:31; Matthew 13:36ff].

Just as Noah's sons' families repopulated the earth after the flood, so the physical citizens of the Kingdom will repopulate the earth after the devastation of the Tribulation. The population of the earth is so great at the end of the thousand years, their numbers are likened to the sand of the sea—innumerable [Revelation 20:8]. Only those in physical bodies can procreate according to God's divine order. Therefore, if the Rapture occurs after the Tribulation, there would be no physical presence left on the earth to repopulate it. All believers would be translated into eternal bodies that do not marry, as the angels do not marry [Matthew 22:30]. There would be no living believers in their physical bodies left on the earth to bear children in the Kingdom.

The children must be born of a surviving Tribulation remnant, those who come to faith in Christ during the seven years but are not members of the Church. They enter the Kingdom in their human bodies and repopulate the earth after the Tribulation. These believers missed the Rapture when the door of the Church Age was closed but they find true salvation in the Tribulation revival. God's grace is still in operation during the Tribulation.

What about a Prewrath or Midtribulation Rapture? There is a view that the Church goes through half of the Tribulation, the half before Antichrist declares himself "god" by erecting an image of himself in the Jewish temple [Revelation 13; Matthew 24: 15; Daniel 11:31; 12:11]. In this view only the second half of the Tribulation is thought to fit the criteria of wrath. Although Antichrist is consolidating his empire in the first half and does not show his full hand until the mid-point, the first half still experiences the opening of God's Seal and Trumpet judgments. In Daniel's prophecy of the seventy weeks, the entire prophecy is "determined" for Israel, not the Church, including the entire portion of the remaining seven years of the prophecy. [Daniel 9:24] The seven years are a unit of the determined time, the only portion of the seventy weeks left to be fulfilled.

All seven are the wrath of God on a Christ-rejecting world, even though the second half is more terrible than the first. The Tribulation is defined as "wrath" as early as the Seal Judgments in Revelation 6:17 – "For the great day of His wrath has come, and who is able to stand?" Chapter six of the Revelation is the unsealing of the Seal judgments, the first event of the first half of the Tribulation, approximately three and a half years before the mid-point of the seven years. Even the early judgments and the false peace of the first half of the Tribulation is God's wrath.

Also, if the Rapture were to occur at the mid-point, every believer would be taken out instantly. How then could there be a Jewish remnant that flees Jerusalem and is protected by God in the wilderness for the last half of the Tribulation? [Revelation 12:13-17] The only logical answer is that the Rapture occurs before the Tribulation begins.

The timing of the Rapture is a tender subject. I was once told those who believe in a Pretribulation Rapture are "copping out," that we are shirking our duty for the "kingdom" by wanting rapture before Tribulation. First, personal preference does not determine God's timing. Second, certainly there are complacent believers. But Pretribulation believers should not be labeled as lazy in doing the Lord's work because we wait in anticipation for His return. Those who have an understanding of the times are often more concerned about living a fruitful and productive Christian life because we are acutely aware He could return at any moment. We know He will require an accounting of what we did to occupy until He comes and we do not want to be found shirking [1 Corinthians 3:11-15; Luke 19:11-27]. I do not teach a Pretribulation Rapture because it is a convenient way to avoid the Tribulation; I teach it because scripture teaches it.

THE TRIBULATION IS DETERMINED FOR ISRAEL

When interpreting prophecy, a clear distinction between the Church and Israel must be maintained [Romans 11]. The Tribulation is not about the Church, it is a vehicle to restore Israel to their Messiah. Look again at Daniel 9:20-27, the prophecy of the Seventy Weeks of Daniel or the Seventy Weeks of Years. In this prophecy God outlines to Daniel the determined time in which He would "finish the transgression" of Daniel's people Israel [9:24]. The majority of the four hundred and ninety years of time in which God would deal directly with Israel has been perfectly fulfilled and historically proven. All that remains is the Tribulation, which will complete the Lord's reconciliation of Israel.

Jeremiah 30:7 – "Alas! For that day is great, so that none is like it; and it is the time of Jacob's trouble, but he shall be saved out of it."

Jacob's descendants are Israel. The Day of the Lord, which includes the tribulation and return of Christ, will be the testing and refining of Israel to bring them to repentance; they will be saved through that testing. Two-thirds of the Jewish people shall die as a result of the Seals, Trumpets and Bowl judgments; but the one-third that comes "through the fire" will call on the name of the Lord [Zechariah 13:8-9]. "And so all Israel will be saved..." [Romans 11:26]; the remnant of believing Israel is the true Israel. The Tribulation is the time of Jacob's or

Israel's trouble, but it is to finally break their hard hearts and bring them to Him.

Not only is the Tribulation to finish the work of Christ for Israel, it is also Christ's defeat of Satan and his followers. A day of literal spiritual warfare between the armies of God and the armies of Satan will be fought in heaven. Satan will be thrown out of God's throne room forever; his territory during the last days of the tribulation will be confined to the earth [Revelation 12:7-9]. At Armageddon he will suffer defeat and be imprisoned in the bottomless pit [Revelation 20:1-3].

The Day of the Lord, the tribulation and return of Christ, is the "storm of the LORD" bursting out in His wrath on the heads of the wicked [Jeremiah 30:23-24]. Isaiah 2:11—"The lofty looks of man shall be humbled, the haughtiness of men shall be bowed down, and the LORD alone shall be exalted in that day."

Because the Church is under no condemnation, what purpose would it serve if we were appointed to a determined time of God's wrath? 1Thessalonians 5:9 – "For God did not appoint us to wrath, but to obtain salvation through our Lord Jesus Christ..."

A passage that clarifies the timing of the Rapture as opposed to the Second Coming is found in 2 Thessalonians 2:1-12. "Our gathering together to Him" refers to the Rapture. Paul explains that the Rapture must occur before the lawless one, Antichrist, can be revealed [verse 8] because such evil cannot manifest itself until He who now restrains is taken out of the way. The question is: Who is the restrainer of evil?

The Holy Spirit indwells every Church Age believer [John 14]. The Spirit, spread abroad in believers, restrains lawlessness. Only after the Rapture when the Church, which is indwelt with the Holy Spirit, is taken from the earth, can lawlessness grow unrestrained and Antichrist come to power. When the Church is present, the salt and light of redemption restrains evil from emerging. Imagine what the world will be like after the Rapture when the earth is devoid of believers for a time. It will rot quickly.

Therefore the Rapture will take place before the Antichrist is allowed to come onto the scene. When does Antichrist appear? He appears as a representative to sign or affirm a treaty with Israel for seven years; it is this event that begins the countdown of the Tribulation [Daniel 9:27].

Finally, if the Church must go through the Tribulation before Christ returns for His bride, why would Titus call the Rapture the blessed hope of the Church? It cannot be a blessed hope if we are waiting for Antichrist and the Tribulation instead of the Bridegroom.

CONFRONTING THE COMING STORM

The only way to defeat fear is to confront it. A storm of immense proportions is coming upon the world. A major war may confront the nations before the Tribulation even begins. Many consider Psalm 83 to be a description of a Middle East war between Israel and their surrounding enemies. War not only is coming; it is erupting in multiple Middle East conflicts. It doesn't work to bury our heads in the sand and go about our earthly business. Denial is human however. God warned that most of the earth will deny reality—as they did in the days of Noah.

The example of the flood in Noah's time is significant because the flood was the first global judgment. It is Christ's specific red flag warning. The world was in denial and caught up in the every-day. They did not know what was happening until the flood took them away [Matthew 24:37-39]. Christ uses the precedent of Noah's time and the flood to demonstrate the prevalent attitude of the end times before the second global judgment.

Being willfully clueless is not new. The Pharisees and Sadducees were rebuked by Jesus for not recognizing the obvious signs of His first coming. "When it is evening you say, 'It will be fair weather, for the sky is red'; and in the morning, 'It will be foul weather today, for the sky is red and threatening.' Hypocrites! You know how to discern the face of the sky, but you cannot discern the signs of the times." [Matthew 16:2-4]

We do not have to be blind to the signs of Christ's return as the lost were in Noah's day [Matthew 24:37-39] or the Pharisees in Christ's day. We have the prophetic Word to inform us of the coming forecast. We are prepared by knowing a storm is heading our way. But after the storm, the clouds will part, the sun will come out, and the Son of Man will descend to the earth in great glory.

As a side note, notice just how literal the Bible is by a simple example. Since I was a child I heard the old saying "Red sky at night, sailor's delight; red sky at morning, sailor take warning." I was told that when an evening sunset was bright red, we could be sure of fair weather the next day; but if the morning sunrise was bright red, a storm was brewing. Being the inquisitive gal I am, I have tested this theory again and again and find that it is always accurate. Imagine my surprise as a young believer when I discovered that this weather forecasting tool originated in the Bible.

A LITERAL INTERPRETATION

The signs of the times are just as literal and are to be used to help us forecast the times in which we live. This in no way means we are to set dates. But we are to be wise. As Daniel was warned, only the wise will really understand what is going on at the time of the end [Daniel 12:4, 10].

The mistake is to take the analogy too far. For example I wanted room in my garden to grow potatoes. I read a pin on Pinterest that said potatoes could be grown in a large barrel. Start with a layer of soil over seed potatoes on the bottom. Then, as they grow, cover up the growth so that more potatoes grow on the next level. Continue to do this until the barrel is filled. Harvest your potatoes when the top growth dies back; enjoy a barrel full of potatoes.

I took these instructions too literally. Instead of just covering up the lower part of the potato plants, I covered the whole plant. Most of the plants died. I harvested only enough potatoes from the barrel to re-plant it again this year. This time I covered only the bottoms of the plants and hope to finally reap a good return.

Look for example at this symbolism in Revelation thirteen. There the Antichrist is described as a monstrous beast with seven heads and ten horns. Will the coming world ruler be a literal monster? When truth is communicated through symbols, those symbols are explained either in the passage itself or in other parts of the Bible. The Word uses heads to represent headship authority. Seven heads are thought to represent seven past empires that were also saturated with the Babylonian Mystery Religion that is the one-world false religion of the Tribulation. Horns in the Bible represent the contemporary authority of this monstrous leader. Daniel tells us his global empire will be served by ten kings, represented by these ten horns of power wearing crowns [Daniel 7:19-24; Revelation 17:12-13]. The Frankenstein monster beast is also said to have body parts like a leopard, a bear, and a lion. These animals represent characteristics of the past world empires of Greece, Persia and Babylon [Daniel 7].

What do we interpret from this? Antichrist is the end times composite of the best and worst of all human power structures—the last global empire of man [Daniel 2]. But when they are assembled together, he and his kingdom resemble a Frankenstein monster and yet he is a man [Daniel 2; 7:24-25; 8:9-12; 23-25; 9:27; 11:36; Revelation 13]. The Beast is a title used to describe both Antichrist and his empire.

Discernment and sound Biblical interpretation is required to interpret the Word of God literally. It is to be *rightly divided*. [2 Timothy 2:15] As a carpenter cuts the wood straight rightly dividing it, so the Word must be interpreted accurately. Just as the prophecies of Christ's first coming as a baby in Bethlehem and as our Savior to die on the cross were literally fulfilled, so His second coming prophecies will be literally fulfilled.

In the coming chapters we will examine passages that specifically apply to what we as believers are to be doing and how we are to be living while waiting in faith and hope for His return. Get ready to pack your spiritual bug-out bag and flex your spiritual muscles.

~

Practical Prepping

My grandmother baked incredible pies. Every slice I encounter is compared to hers. Some years ago I determined to become as good a pie maker as my grandmother. For a year I worked to find the right recipe for pastry and perfected the art of flaky pie crust.

Now my husband and kids tell me my pies are "the best." They do at times rise up and call me blessed. Setting myself tasks that require discipline and improvement are good for me. Although I am not changing the world, it makes me feel more grounded in the one I have been given to occupy.

The Lord is with me in my kitchen. When I am canning or baking I listen to Bible study CDs from favorite teachers and feed my mind while I am cooking for my family.

It has been a great blessing to invite young women into my kitchen and teach them how to bake a pie completely from scratch. Mentoring does not have to be a formal affair. It is as simple as sharing the joy of a beautifully browned crust and bubbling filling.

~

4

SHADOWS OF THE FOUR HORSEMEN OF THE APOCALYPSE

Are you aware Christ sent the Church a personal letter? The book of The Revelation is addressed to Christ's Church through seven letters to seven churches in Asia Minor. Through these seven early churches this letter was to be read to all known churches of the day and the Church throughout time.

The Revelation of Jesus Christ is still addressed to His Church but few congregations read it or teach it. If you received a special delivery letter from Christ that was stamped "urgent" on the front, wouldn't you be curious about what information the letter contained? The Lord always warns before judgment and the Revelation reveals important information to prepare the Church for what is to come.

The Revelation is the only book in the Bible that promises a blessing to those who read it, hear it, and keep it "for the time is near." [Revelation 1:2] Personally, I want to receive all the blessings the Lord has provided; and yet many Christians consider the book irrelevant. I can attest to the fact that the study of prophecy has abundantly increased my faith, hope, wisdom and spiritual discernment beyond my human capacity. It has been invaluable.

The Revelation also contains a curse for those who edit it by adding things that are not there or taking away what *is* there. To consider the book merely a symbolic struggle between good and evil and not a literal revealing of future events edits it. To consider the book a cryptic account of events that have already been fulfilled is to take away its preparation for Christ's return [Revelation 22:18-19].

The apathy of the Church in the end times is no surprise to our Lord; He prophesied that it would come. He ends each of the messages in Revelation chapters two and three with these words: "He who has an ear, let him hear what the Spirit says to the churches." [Revelation 2:11] He doesn't expect the majority of His Church to listen because of stifling apostasy, which is a falling away from the faith. "Now the Spirit expressly says that in latter times some will depart from the faith, giving heed to deceiving spirits and doctrines of demons..." [1 Timothy 4:1] [See also 2 Timothy 3:5; 4:3-4]. Christ's earnest plea to those who have an ear to hear echoes from His heart today and yet His Church is willfully ignorant of future things.

For example, those who believe the unrest in the world will get better as Christianity takes over may not find a view to their liking in this book. Those in denial about the state of world affairs are certainly not reading prophecy. Like a watcher on the wall, this is a wake-up call to Christians who are not hearing what His Word is saying. Pandemic change is operating in virtually every dimension of human existence with an obvious conclusion; global conditions are becoming progressively worse. 2 Timothy 3:13—"But evil men and impostors will grow worse and worse, deceiving and being deceived."

Daniel 12:4 describes the time of the end as a state of frenzy accompanied by the exponential increase in knowledge. Few would deny that chaos is a good word to describe the times in which we live. Some believe it is ordered chaos that will eventually lead to utopia; but chaos destined to become worse and worse is in no way ordered. It is becoming progressively uncontrollable until the signs of the times coalesce into the opening judgments of the Tribulation—The Seal Judgments [Revelation 6].

Technological advances are touted as human accomplishments that point to man's continuing evolution. But a humanity that cannot keep up with its own ingenuity only creates chaos. Can we put to rest the well-meaning but misguided notion that things are getting better? Paul warned the Thessalonians that the mystery of lawlessness was already at work in his day [2 Thessalonians 2:7]. Imagine what the world will be like when the salt and light of the church is taken out at the Rapture and the world is allowed to rot without restraint. Darkness will overtake any semblance of light. If lawlessness operated in Paul's day and continues to the present, we should be witnessing lawless trends increasing in frequency and intensity—and indeed we do.

We are seeing a foreshadowing of the Seals now—not a fulfillment, only a preview of coming events. Like birth pains, they will become increasingly more intense and more frequent as the Day of the Lord, the return of Christ, nears [Matthew 24:8]. Although the world has seen terrible times, never before have we witnessed the signs increasing in frequency and intensity to this degree, like labor pains pushing toward deliverance. This is a point I make to believers who are passive about the signs of the times because of date setters and extremists. Note carefully: It is Christ's qualifier of labor pains that identifies signs of His return from other cataclysmic events in history. He said general signs would herald His return when they increase exponentially, becoming radically more frequent and more intense, like the pains of a woman in labor. This is what we are witnessing.

The return of Israel to their ancestral land and the re-establishment of Israel as a nation in 1948 was also a definitive signal. The Tribulation and return of Christ cannot be fulfilled unless Israel is in the land and has possession of The Temple Mount. As the Lord said, when the fig free, which is symbolic of Israel, puts forth leaves again, His return is "at the doors!" "Assuredly, I say to you, this generation will by no means pass away till all these things take place. Heaven and earth will pass away, but My words will by no means pass away." [Matthew 24:32-35]

I was born one year after Israel became a nation again, a miracle of history. No other nation has been reborn in their ancestral territory with an intact race, language and religion. In in their dispersion, the Lord was a sanctuary to them to protect them as a race until their return to Israel, the land [Ezekiel 11:16-17].

All these things are shadows of events to come that the Church of Jesus Christ must recognize and confront using every weapon of practical Christianity at our disposal. Otherwise, we cannot be mentally and spiritually prepared for His any-moment return. Look with me at the general signs that Christ Jesus gave us.

A REVEALING COMPARISON OF MATTHEW 24:4-8 AND REVELATION 6:1-8: Matthew 24 was a teaching given by our Lord as an overview of His Second Coming. Verses four to eight are considered general signs that are part of this increasing lawlessness that will eventually culminate in the Seals of the Tribulation and the judgments that follow them. They parallel the first four Seals—the four horsemen of the apocalypse— very closely.

SEAL ONE: Antichrist, the rider on the white horse who promises peace and safety, is the first Seal judgment. He is the climax of the deceivers, false prophets and false christs our Lord warned of in Matthew 24:4-5. In the Tribulation, Antichrist is the zenith of lawlessness—he is called "the lawless one" [2 Thessalonians 2:9]. Antichrist will blatantly demand that he operate above the law—any law. Many false teachers are even now deceiving apostate church attenders but the Antichrist is Satan's star pupil. In the Tribulation, Antichrist will employ false signs and lying wonders to accompany his promises to save the world. Those who gauge what to believe by emotion instead of truth will be easily led astray.

Deceptive, lying leaders are prevalent in our time; we have no need to argue the point. But the most distressing reality is that the majority of constituents believe the lies in spite of all evidence to the contrary. Isaiah wrote that evil would be sold as good and good as evil to a corrupt people [Isaiah 5]. Clearly common sense and truth have been turned upside down and have become inverse morality. It is not logical to deny a standard of morality and absolute truth, but that is exactly what lawlessness demands.

SEAL TWO: The red horse or the second Seal is war and bloodshed. Antichrist, who gains power by promising peace, quickly leads the world into the most terrible state of war ever imagined. The War of Armageddon will end only when Christ returns at the culminating Battle of Armageddon [Revelation 19; Zechariah 14]. "For when they say, 'Peace and safety!' then sudden destruction comes upon them, as labor pains upon a pregnant woman. And they shall not escape." [1 Thessalonians 5:3] Those who follow the false peace gurus will be desperately unprepared when war encompasses the world.

Contemporary media is hesitant to label any conflict a war—they are called incursions, civil unrest, conflict, confrontations, and any number of descriptive terms for "wars and rumors of war" as our Lord called this sign in Matthew 24:6.

Are we seeing promises of peace where there is no peace in our day? The Arab revolts which were taken over by Islamic terrorist groups were euphemistically labeled "the Arab Spring." These uprisings have plunged Syria, Libya, Egypt and Iraq into war. Africa is in turmoil from radical terrorist groups. Afghanistan is unstable even after years of U.S. presence. Ukraine is being threatened with a Russian takeover. Gaza and Israel are in an unstable cease fire after yet another period of open conflict and yet politicians ceaselessly call for "peace in the Middle East."

Ecumenical movements are also calling for world peace which they believe can be achieved through religious unity. There will be no peace until the Prince of Peace returns to establish it. Diplomacy will fail. Even Antichrist's false peace with Israel, which is the event that opens the Tribulation [Daniel 9:27], will be broken after three and a half years.

SEAL THREE: The black horse represents famine, inflation and starvation. There is much we can speculate about Revelation 6:5-6. America is one of the few remaining capitalistic, wealth-generating nations in the world and our free enterprise is being limited by increasing socialistic laws and government restrictions. When Antichrist institutes the Mark of the Beast, 666, no one will be able to buy or sell without receiving this brand of allegiance to him and his Beast system. His system is not free enterprise. It is socialism, communism or totalitarianism. Because the "whole world" will follow after the Beast, this includes the United States [Revelation 13]. Our free enterprise days are numbered.

Matthew 24:7 also prophesies that conditions leading to famine will increase in frequency and intensity around the globe as the black horse approaches. Wage earners will be unable to buy quality food [wheat] for their families; their income will allow them only enough to buy what was considered animal feed in Christ's day [barley]. The example of the elderly poor living on dog food may be a real possibility in the famine conditions of the Tribulation if not before. But the gap between the extremely wealthy and the poor will remain. It is not just capitalism that creates a wealthy elite—those who consume "the oil and the wine." A privileged class of wealthy bureaucrats exists in even communist governments that preach equality of the masses. They survive by feeding off the poor majority.

Are we seeing a foreshadowing of global economic stress even now? This is another point we do not need to argue if practical observation is applied. Globalists are calling for a one-world economy to solve the massive debt problem. The death of the dollar is thought to be a foregone conclusion; America's loss of economic power will ultimately result in the dollar losing its status as the world's reserve currency. America is not only being devalued morally, it will be devalued economically. The symbolic meaning of the scales and healthy food as compared to animal fodder indicates that wages cannot compete with cost or supply. This is a graphic picture of runaway inflation. Food prices will continue to go up, especially quality food prices, while wages remain the same or fall. A tipping point is rapidly approaching.

California and the western section of the U.S. is undergoing terrible drought conditions, limiting our formerly abundant domestic produce. A disease in the citrus crops in

Florida threatens to destroy that industry. With unrest between nations, sanctions are being leveled against our own nation as we in turn place trade sanctions on others.

What should a practical Christian do? Prepare to diversify and cast your bread on many waters. Our grandparents would say "Don't put all your eggs in one basket." We can take our lessons from the effects of rationing in the great wars and "making do" in the Great Depression. In other words, make the best use of what we have and limit waste. Although we will not be on the earth during the black horse seal, a wise steward prepares for uncertain times. Global economics are sure to falter long before the one-world economy of Antichrist takes over. Ultimately and always, our faith must be in Christ and not our 401K.

SEAL FOUR: "So I looked, and behold, a pale horse. And the name of him who sat on it was Death, and Hades followed with him." [Revelation 6:8]

The fourth horseman is Death, followed closely by Hades or Hell. This is grace as it may indicate that the death totals will hit lost humanity the hardest, those destined for Hell. The death totals of the Seals are an accumulation of all four of the horses: deception leading to war, famine, and finally death. In Matthew 24:7, our Lord mentions "famines, pestilences, and earthquakes in various places." Revelation 6:8 lists death by "sword, with hunger, with death, and by the beasts of the earth."

It is this pale horse that is exciting attention because of the growing possibility of pandemic pestilences. The "beasts of the earth" could broadly refer to microbial bacteria becoming epidemic globally. We have had outbreaks of bird flu, swine flu,

MERSA and now Ebola. The Ebola outbreak is spreading in Africa but historically it will not remain there, in spite of measures we take to confine it. In these days of global travel and leaky borders, pandemic global pestilence is a very real possibility.

The horsemen launch the first half of the Tribulation. With at least three and one-half years yet to be played out, one-fourth of the earth's population will die from the accumulated results of war, famine, natural disasters such as earthquakes in unexpected and random places, and pestilences. Like the ripples in a pond when the stone is cast, the consequences of man's attempts to rule the earth without God create natural consequences of devastating proportions.

GRACE FOR THE REMNANT

Now is the time to be wise in the Word as Daniel warned in Daniel 12:10. The clueless and self-absorbed will be like those asleep when all these things fall upon them. Our blessed hope is to live in expectation of His return and to know what He has revealed about the times of the end. We are not uninformed about what is coming; we need not be unprepared physically, mentally, emotionally or spiritually. This book is written to discuss the practical application of a *vibrant living faith* in Jesus Christ applied to what we know from His Word.

Luke 21:34-36—"But take heed to yourselves, lest your hearts be weighed down with carousing, drunkenness, and cares of this life, and that Day come on you unexpectedly. For it will come as a snare on all those who dwell on the face of the whole earth. Watch therefore, and pray always that you may be counted worthy to escape all these things that will come to pass, and to stand before the Son of Man."

Those of the remnant who have an eye to see and an ear to hear what our Lord is saying to the Church in these days will find this an enticing, demanding, and utterly thrilling time in which to live.

~

Practical Prepping

Those bits of left-over bread or rolls don't have to go to waste. I put them in freezer bags until I have enough to make sage stuffing or cinnamon bread pudding for Sunday dinner.

It is also less expensive to buy a whole stalk of celery than celery hearts. I use what I need for a recipe then cut up the rest and put it in freezer bags. Then when I need celery for stir fry or soup, I have it handy without having to buy another stalk. As veggies accumulate in the freezer, make vegetable soup or stew.

If you have lots of produce from your garden at different times of the season, accumulate recipes to use it and store it. When the tomatoes begin to come on, I have more than we can eat fresh so I can salsa and tomato sauce using fresh herbs. When the apples are coming down in bushels, I can applesauce, apple pie filling, apple butter and I freeze apple slices for pies, breads and crisps. My husband and I would also like to find a reasonable cider press to begin making our own cider and vinegar. Vinegar with the natural yeast is extremely healthy. I also use vinegar for cleaning.

One of the joys of gardening is having friends over for apple picking. I can't think of a more pleasant way to spend a September day.

5

STORM CLOUDS ON THE HORIZON

"But know this, that in the last days perilous times will come: For men will be lovers of themselves..." [2 Timothy 3:1-2]

Self-centered, entitled, narcissistic, selfish—these adjectives describe someone who is a lover of himself. How can we prepare for a worsening of the greed and pride that is destroying our Judeo/Christian culture? Lessons from the past can help us prepare for the future, both our own past and Bible history. Our Lord uses trials and testing to teach us valuable lessons if we have an eye to see.

I was thirteen at the time of the Cuban Missile Crisis. I remember the tension and sitting in front of a black and white television watching as President John F. Kennedy somberly informed the nation that the United States and Russia were in a stand-off, perilously close to targeting each other with nuclear warheads.

During the Cold War families built bomb shelters in their back yards. As a promotion a company constructed an underground shelter in a nearby town and asked for a volunteer family to live in it for a month. A microphone inside was piped to a speaker so that visitors could listen to their conversations. It was surreal. In God's sovereign will, the bombs did not go off in 1962.

Storm clouds are again on the horizon and the forecast is ominous. It is no longer a Cold War limited to two super powers; several nations currently have nuclear arsenals. Especially concerning are the hundreds of nuclear armaments that could easily fall into the hands of radical factions such as Islamic nations or groups fighting for global domination and the restoration of an Islamic Caliphate. Their willingness to do whatever it takes to achieve their zealous goals is a real danger to global security. Threats of invasion and force against Israel and any other power that might object are a common occurrence.

How is the remnant to live in such a time as this? Is the answer to build more bomb shelters? During the tribulation, the lost will indeed attempt to hide in the ground. They cry to the mountains and rocks, "Fall on us and hide us from the face of Him who sits on the throne and from the wrath of the Lamb! For the great day of His wrath has come, and who is able to stand?" [Revelation 6:16-17] The irony is that the lost recognize that the Lamb of God is the source of wrath but they put their hope in the caves to save them rather than the Savior.

The question *who can stand* is immediately answered in Revelation 7. Those that stand triumphantly in the Tribulation are the sealed of Christ, the true believers. Bomb shelters cannot withstand the wrath of God. Only the blood of Christ can truly deliver us from the tribulation to come—or from our present trials for that matter. Without a spiritual bomb shelter, protection in the end times is as ineffective as grade school atomic bomb drills when we were told to hide under our desks for shelter.

A BABY BOOMER'S PERSPECTIVE OF THE END TIMES

As a woman who was born of the greatest generation, I was taught to be self-reliant and strong in the face of adversity. Being self-reliant is vastly different than being self-centered. I learned to garden and cook from scratch, tools that have been very useful and may be even more necessary in the future. I would ask my grandmother what it was like living during the Great Depression. At that time my grandparents lived on a farm outside of town. She said folks in town had more difficulty than those in the country because they were not as self-sustaining as farmers. Farmers tended large gardens and raised chickens and cows. Neighbors helped each other and relatives were often close by. Grandmother recalled a family in their area that was too proud to ask for help. They survived one winter by living on nothing but apples and popcorn.

It is not feasible for wise stewards to all begin farming or homesteading, but there are practical things we can do to adjust for changing times. The key is to know changing times are coming.

World War II followed the Great Depression. I am a baby boomer born in 1949, a few years after the war ended. My father named me for Sharon Kanoa Bay on the island of Saipan where he was stationed. I listened to his stories of war in the South Pacific and heard adults speak of food rationing and blackout drills and the many young men in high school yearbooks who were never coming home. The war years seem far removed from this current generation; wars are fought on other continents, not native soil. It was not so on 9-11 and may not always be so. Let the older women teach the younger that the past has lessons the detached must learn.

The war taught us to bring self-reliance into the city. Families on the home front bought war bonds and planted victory gardens in back yards. The more food the home front could raise for its own use, the more commercial food could go to the troops in Europe. Civilians were forced to be resourceful in order to help the war effort. The old saying *make it do, wear it out, use it up, do without* was practiced by everyone. Tires were patched and dresses were handed down. Can we survive without a mall?

Housewives learned to extend a half pound of ground meat with oatmeal and eggs to feed a family. They called it meat loaf. My grandmother still made her own soap from lye and animal fat when I was in grade school. She drained drippings and collected them in a glass jar shaped like a red apple; it was called a grease saver. Those large creamy yellow bars of soap were used for everything from laundry to scrubbing grandchildren behind the ears. My mother sewed dresses of feed sack calico and I was delighted with the bright colors and fanciful prints. It did not matter to me that the cheap cloth came from chicken feed bags.

I lived through the Cold War. I remember walking down the hall in high school and hearing shouts that President Kennedy had been shot. I watched my brother leave for Viet Nam and after college met and married another Viet Nam vet. And then the towers fell. "Wars and rumors of wars" have become a constant reality [Matthew 24:6] as the prophetic Word tells us leading many to become dangerously complacent. The Middle East is a powder keg destined to ignite. This is the very real possibility this generation faces.

THE LIGHT OF PROPHECY

I am grateful for the practical knowledge I have accumulated in my lifetime. But hard work and personal experience is not enough to prepare for the times ahead if persecution increases on the home front before the Rapture. The ultimate answer is not a crash course in survival methods.

The answer is to develop discernment and spiritual wisdom and to live by faith and hope. God speaks through His Son, the living Word, in these last days [Hebrews 1:2; 1 John 1:1] Daniel was told to close up his prophetic book and seal it until the time of the end because the fulfillment was not for his time. It was for the time when people would be running around frantically and knowledge would increase exponentially. We have arrived at that level of chaos.

The book closes with these words: "Many shall be purified made white, and refined, but the wicked shall do wickedly; and none of the wicked shall understand, *but the wise shall understand."* [Daniel 12:10 emphasis mine]

As a young woman I did not have the spiritual discernment to understand the implications of God's sovereign control of history. We were clueless denominational christians when my husband and I were married and were more occupied with work and adjusting to life together than attending church regularly. After a home visit by two of our church elders I was convicted to worship consistently but still limited my religion to Sunday morning.

We took notice of the committed behavior of a Godly couple in the congregation. I became hungry for the kind of personal relationship with Christ they demonstrated. I gave myself completely to Christ Jesus and received Him by grace through faith as Lord and Savior; my husband did the same one week later. For the first time I was filled with a need to read the Bible. The light began to come on.

One Sunday evening my life was radically changed for the second time. My husband and I attended a movie night at the church sponsored by our mentoring couple. The film was *A*

Thief in the Night, a prophecy movie produced over forty years ago. I sat mesmerized as the plot depicted what life could be like in the days leading up to the Pretribulation Rapture. As we drove home I told my husband, "If there is such a thing as the Rapture in the Bible, I need to know."

Curiosity became a hunger for truth. I studied Bible prophecy intensely and discovered the Word does indeed describe the moment when Christ will descend in the clouds and catch out the Church. In the mainline denomination in which I was raised, I was not taught a literal Rapture or a literal seven-year Tribulation or a literal thousand-year earthly kingdom called the Millennium. The return of Christ was spoken of vaguely as something that would happen at the end of time, the end of the world or someday. The book of the Revelation was thought to be a symbolic portrayal of the struggle between good and evil. In other words, they did not interpret it literally. The culminating book of the Bible was not considered terribly relevant, even though it is God's last word to His Church. It is indeed a book using many symbols but they are symbols with a literal meaning. The final battle is coming but God wins the war!

THE MYSTERY OF LAWLESSNESS – WORSE AND WORSE

Studying prophecy as literal scripture with a future fulfillment leads to a timeline with an obvious conclusion as we have seen. When sailing unfamiliar waters, it is essential to have a map. Bible prophecy provides that map to help us navigate while conditions worsen before Christ's return. In my sixty-five years I have witnessed the decline of our nation and increasing lawlessness on a global scale. Clearly the political, social, cultural and religious world is growing worse and worse—I can testify to living through rapid and definitive deterioration.

Immorality is not only accepted in the misguided name of rights and freedom, laws are being written to condone it. This is the slide into depravity Paul warned about in Romans 1:18-32.

It is also essential to face reality rather than live in denial of the truth. Understanding that things are becoming progressively worse is crucial to wise discernment. Those who ignore the obvious will be unprepared for the coming days. It may be all they can do to hold their own houses together and will be of no help to other believers.

Look again at Paul's letter to the Thessalonians. He told them that not only is the mystery of lawlessness already at work, he also revealed that the Holy Spirit restrains this lawlessness from taking complete control...until. Until what? Until the Holy Spirit is taken out of the way in the Rapture [2 Thessalonians 2:7]. As the Lord explained in John 14, God's power in the Church is spread abroad because believers are indwelt by the Holy Spirit. That widespread power does much to restrain evil while the Church is on the earth. During the Tribulation the Holy Spirit will still be *with* the believers as He was in the Old Testament, but He is no longer *in* them.

The evil we see now is nothing in comparison to the unrestrained lawlessness after the Rapture. Even now the remnant of preserving salt and exposing light of the Church is fighting against a generation of narcissistic, entitled people who think only of themselves. [2 Timothy 3:1-2] When society is fueled by self-gratification, it is little wonder Paul said the last days would be perilous times in which to live. We live in those perilous times now.

How then should the Church prepare? If the Rapture is our blessed hope, should we sit around on the porch doing nothing but waiting? Prophecy students are at times accused of doing just that because we rightly believe the Rapture is indeed our blessed hope. But the Lord doesn't intend for His Church to sit around on their hands in the meantime. Spiritual prepping does require equipment and effort.

When rebuilding the walls of Jerusalem after the Babylonian captivity, the strength of the laborers had been failing due to the enormity of the task and the threat of attack from Israel's enemies. Nehemiah the governor came to Israel with a burden to see that the work was finished. He scouted the city at night in order to determine the magnitude of the project and hide his plans from spies. The threat to those building was so great, Nehemiah positioned armed guards with drawn swords, spears and bows to stand by the workers in order to protect them while they worked.

Nehemiah knew the God of Israel was behind the work but the people needed to invest themselves in it by standing, fighting and working with Nehemiah. The governor arose and said, "Do not be afraid of them. Remember the Lord, great and awesome, and fight for your brethren, your sons, your daughters, your wives, and your houses." [Nehemiah 2:12-16; 4:10-15]

The Church must know that our occupation in this life will increasingly require drawn swords and a courageous spirit as part of our spiritual armor. We must constantly keep watch and scout the enemy in order to defend our positions and fight for truth. Our battles may be more spiritual than physical, but they are just as real. Prepare for the battle to become worse as the Tribulation nears. "And then the lawless one will be revealed, whom the Lord will consume with the breath of His mouth and destroy with the brightness of His coming." [2 Thessalonians 2:8]

~

Practical Prepping

The Cottage Garden

Most of my garden is dedicated to things we like to eat. A good way to save on groceries is to grow it yourself. But flowers are a smile among the vegetables. I plant mostly perennial flowers rather than annuals because they come back every season. We have accumulated peonies, iris, astilbe, daisies, sea lavender, mums, knockout roses, hydrangea, oriental lilies, artemisia, yellow yarrow and sedum. Perennials need only be planted once for a lifetime of color. Most of my perennials were gifts from other gardeners who had plenty to share and I share mine as well.

Perennial wild flowers are also a wonderful addition in a casual cottage garden. These I dug from woods and road sides in Illinois. I have wild violets, goldenrod, Illinois sun flowers, white yarrow, phlox, field lilies, Queen Ann's Lace, sour dock and bee balm. In the bare spots I sow zinnia and marigold seeds saved from previous year's blooms.

The self-seeding annuals and biennials sow themselves, which is very nice of them. I discover celosia, sweet Annie Artemisia, hollyhocks and sweet William scattered here and there in the spring. Some bloom where they take root and others I transplant. Cottage gardening makes the most of what earth you have, grouping fruits, vegetables, flowers and herbs together in a cozy tumble.

6

HIS SOVEREIGN PURPOSE

There is an answer for every hard spiritual question. What is that answer? All is for the glory of God. We exist for the glory of God [Isaiah 43:7]. All things were created through Him and for Him to bring Him glory and in Him they continue to exist [Colossians 1:16]. He is the super glue that holds everything together. The resolution of history in the end times raises questions the human mind finds difficult to answer. Coming to an understanding of God's sovereign purpose in the coming wrath will equip us for the Lord's return by preparing us to give Him glory.

Why is our merciful God allowing His creation to deteriorate? How can a loving God allow the death toll and destruction of the Tribulation? To bring glory to His name, the Lord is letting sinful man reap what he has sown. He is allowing man to have everything he thinks he wants including freedom from God's restraining laws.

The coming wrath of the Tribulation does not negate the long-suffering mercy of our Lord; He has already patiently offered His grace through ages of time: innocence, conscience, human government, promise, law/Israel, and grace/Church. This is dispensational truth spanning thousands of years and the Kingdom age is yet to follow. For the most part only a remnant comes to Christ in any age; many are called but few are chosen. Man has failed every test—even this dispensation of unmerited favor called the age of grace. The Tribulation is another vehicle of grace, but this time through His wrath. Man has had every opportunity to believe and yet he rebels against God; wrath is God's most severe attempt to bring him to his knees so the only way he has to look is up. Hearts will either harden or break open for Christ during the Tribulation.

"The coming of the lawless one is according to the working of Satan, with all power, signs, and lying wonders, and with all unrighteous deception among those who perish, because they did not receive the love of the truth, that they might be saved. And for this reason God will send them strong delusion, that they should believe the lie, that they all may be condemned who did not believe the truth but had pleasure in unrighteousness." [2 Thessalonians 2:9-12]

The lost want to believe Satan's lies; the Lord will make it easy for them by aiding the delusion. Sinful man is allowed to convict himself so that he will have no excuse before the Great White Throne Judgment of the lost. [Revelation 20:11-15] Those who reject our Lord will find their name is not written in the Lamb's Book of Life; this proves they did not receive Christ and His salvation. No argument will stand against that written proof, even a list of their so-called "good works." But the works of the lost as like filthy rags to Christ and will also be rejected. Their day in court vindicates and glorifies our merciful Judge and convicts the guilty before they are sentenced to the Lake of Fire, eternal Hell. There is a divine purpose in it all which is revealed in His Word.

God sovereignly allows the Tribulation balance of judgment and mercy for His glory and the outworking of His divine truth. As I observe festering evil, I have the comfort of knowing He is in control and will culminate history in His time with a dramatic and satisfying victory.

The Revelation explains it this way. The Lord is allowing sin to ripen and reach its zenith; then He will harvest the lost like plump ripe grapes in a wine press. Waiting for evil to climax allows judgment to be that much more dramatic. "And the winepress was trampled outside the city, and blood came out of the winepress, up to the horses' bridles, for one thousand six hundred furlongs." [Revelation 14:20] The blood flow is described as being four feet deep and running the length of Israel, so great is the slaughter of those who war against God. The blood will channel down the trench of the Jordan River into the Dead Sea. The blood of the spiritually dead stagnates in the Dead Sea because the Sea is below sea level and has no outlet. What a fitting tomb for the dross of man's rebellion against God—fitting also because the Dead Sea is the tomb of what was once known as Sodom and Gomorrah.

The Lord is magnificent in His poetic justice; every action is orchestrated to demonstrate His divine glory. This basin of blood will be cleansed by a kind of artesian well that supernaturally gushes from under the threshold of Christ's new Millennial Temple, the center of worship in Christ's earthly Kingdom. [Ezekiel 47:1-8] This new water source will cause the Dead Sea to overflow and begin emptying into the Gulf of Aqaba. What a picture of holy cleansing—cleansing that was available to the lost if only they would have accepted it.

"Then he said to me; 'This water flows toward the eastern region, goes down into the valley, and enters the sea. When it reaches the sea, its waters are healed.'" Our Lord, the source of living water that springs up into everlasting life as He told the woman at the well [John 4:13-14], literally and physically demonstrates His supernatural power by causing His temple water to cleanse Israel after Armageddon. The wilderness is watered so that it blossoms as the rose [Isaiah 35:1]. Just as we are raised from death to life at salvation, so the remnant of the Tribulation will see the earth spiritually and physically reborn after the destruction of the Seals, Trumpets and Bowl judgments. The destruction and death is healed, not to the condition of before the Tribulation but to the pristine perfection of Eden [Ezekiel 36:35]. Believers of all ages will enjoy His lush earthly Kingdom for one thousand years. Those who died as martyrs are raised to everlasting life bearing the eternal honor of dying for him. It is all about the display of His sovereignty over His own creation. It is for His glory.

The wrath that is poured out like water from the judgments during those seven years results in the death of half of the world's population: a fourth as a result of the Seal judgments [Revelation 6:8] and another third as a result of the Trumpet judgments [Revelation 9:15]. The Tribulation is filled with righteous justice. Man elevates the environment to a religion, arrogantly believing he can save a planet he did not create and cannot control. To display God's control over that which He created, the Lord allows the judgments of the Trumpets to destroy one-third of the green vegetation, one-third of the seas or salt water, and one-third of the fresh water.[Revelation 8:7-11] He elevates the judgment in the Bowls by completely polluting all salt water and by completely polluting all fresh water. [Revelation 16:3-7] Man is helpless to prevent it.

The plagues that God rained down on Egypt were also divinely inspired to curse Pharaoh's people with the very things they worshipped in their pagan religious system. They worshipped the Nile, so God turned it to blood in the first plague. Every plague Moses called forth symbolized another Egyptian deity: frogs, lice, flies, livestock disease, boils, hail, locusts and darkness. The Egyptians worshipped Ra the god of

79

the sun; God plunged them into darkness [Exodus 7:20-10:22]. The power of Ra was made a laughingstock in the face of the Son of God.

Our Lord is long-suffering and merciful but He is also holy and just. During the seven mercifully short years of the Tribulation He returns to take from Satan that which He purchased with His blood. He rescues His believing remnant and His creation that was cursed in Adam's fall. [Romans 8:18-22] His dramatic return in power will literally flatten and dissolve His enemies, vividly demonstrating His superior claim. "And this shall be the plague with which the LORD will strike all the people who fought against Jerusalem: Their flesh shall dissolve while they stand on their feet, their eyes shall dissolve in their sockets, and their tongues shall dissolve in their mouths." [Zechariah 14:12]

In response to the works of Christ in judgment, His saints in heaven, including the Raptured/Resurrected Church before His throne, will worship Him: "...Great and marvelous are Your works, Lord God Almighty! Just and true are Your ways, O King of the saints! Who shall not fear You, O Lord, and glorify Your name? For You alone are holy. For all nations shall come and worship before You, for Your judgments have been manifested." [Revelation 15:3-4, The song of Moses and the Lamb]

Our God is to be glorified, not questioned.

A REVEALING POINT OF VIEW

The question of whether things are getting better or worse is also an aid to reveal a person's view on the end times. I have asked Christian leaders if they believe things are getting worse or better. Some optimistically answered that things may look bad but they are bound to get better because they believe the Church has replaced Israel in God's plan of the ages. This is called Replacement Theology. Now that the Church has taken over where Israel failed, they reason, they are confident the Church will evangelize the world before Christ returns. When the world becomes *Christian,* they naturally believe the world must get better.

Replacement Theology wrongly teaches that the Church must fulfill Israel's role in God's plan because Israel has been cut off forever and their purpose must be fulfilled by their replacement, the Church. Sadly this view is gaining popularity in evangelical denominations. In order to appropriate Israel's blessings they interpret the word Israel to mean the Church in prophetic scriptures; but this is not interpreting the Word literally. When interpreting the Bible literally, Israel simply means Israel and the Church means the Church. The Bible must be interpreted literally in order for God's purpose to be correctly revealed. Just as Christ's first coming was literally fulfilled, so His second coming will be literally fulfilled.

If the Lord has replaced Israel in His plan of the ages, then the unconditional covenant promises God made to Abraham and his descendants are no longer binding. God made a contract with Israel to give them a land, a people and a king in the line of David; the fulfillment of these promises is yet future. God cut the covenant with Abraham alone, sealing it by His own word. [Genesis 15] If God were to forsake Israel forever and not uphold His contract, He would be breaking His own word. For a holy, righteous God, that is impossible. Israel's promises do not belong to the Church and their purpose will not be accomplished by the Church. The Church has its own calling as the Bride of Christ [Ephesians 5:22-32] which is fulfilled at the Rapture.

Paul explains in Romans chapter eleven that Israel has been cast away for a time for rejecting their King when He first appeared; however, they will be grafted back into His plan. [Romans 11:1-27] Daniel chapter nine reveals even more—that the final stage of God's dealing with Israel is a seven year period called the Seventieth Week of Daniel. Several issues listed in Daniel must be resolved with Israel and only with Israel in the seven year Tribulation. To confirm that the Tribulation is designed to restore Israel, Jeremiah the prophet called the Tribulation "the time of Jacob's trouble, but he shall be saved out of it." [Jeremiah 30:7] Jeremiah used Israel's tribal root name to affirm the prophet was speaking of the race of Jews and not the entity known as the Church.

If the Church cries "foul" because they accuse Israel of crucifying our God, remember that He died for our sins as well as theirs. Sinful mankind put Christ on the cross; Israel and the Roman Empire were merely vehicles of His divine plan. Israel will be restored as God's chosen people during the Millennial Kingdom.

If the Church is so anxious to appropriate Israel's role, perhaps they should also appropriate Israel's chastening during the Tribulation. In order to purge Israel and turn them to their God, He refines them in the fire of His wrath. Two-thirds of the Jews in the land shall die; only one-third shall survive. Only then will God say "This is My people; and each one will say, 'The Lord is my God." [Zechariah 13:8-9]

Replacement Theology is taking the evangelical Church down another slippery slope because it is often coupled with an agenda of world peace through the unity of world faiths. Unity is seen as a vehicle to facilitate global evangelism in a pragmatic "the end justifies the means" method. Global evangelism is perceived as the mandate of the church to Christianize the world in order to establish the kingdom for Christ, not as an ongoing work of spreading the Gospel and witnessing to the truth [Acts 1:8]. But it is not the work of the Church to establish the Millennial Kingdom; it is the work of the King when He returns.

The Church, with misplaced zeal, is promoting false teaching because in order for denominations and varied religions of the world to unite, truth must be compromised. The result is a false religious system based on pragmatic programs, not truth. False religion does not bring world peace or Christianity. Is the global ecumenical movement promoting the return of Christ or enabling the false religion of Antichrist?

In Revelation chapter seventeen, prophecy reveals that a global false religious system will indeed exist; it will be consolidated in the Tribulation and run by the Antichrist's false prophet after the true Church is taken out. [Revelation 13; 17] This Tribulation religion does not worship the one true God. God calls it the Babylonian Mystery Religion, a harlot religion because of its long history of demonism, occult deception and paganism. This mother goddess/child cult originated at the Tower of Babel in Babylon and has produced many offspring. It is the seed of all false religion that spread throughout the world after the flood.

That bad seed continues to grow fervently in our nation and the world today. Its followers are obsessed with occult signs, miracles, mysticism, and emotionalism without the substance of truth. "Now the Spirit expressly says that in latter times some will depart from the faith, giving heed to deceiving spirits and doctrines of demons..." [1 Timothy 4:1]

Another deception that is steering some in the Church away from God's purpose involves the coming Kingdom. The Kingdom on earth is yet future. Kingdom Now, Dominion Theology and other similar errors teach that the Lord's earthly Kingdom was established at Christ's first coming and that it became the mandate of the Church to complete His work by evangelizing the world and making it Christian. This teaching stems from a wrong interpretation of the Great Commission in Matthew 28. The Lord did not tell the disciples to convert the world; He told them to be ongoing witnesses of Him wherever He would send them. Conversion is the work of the Holy Spirit. Our work is to witness to the truth and make disciples just as He did. Although He will return as King, He came first to bear witness to the truth and it is truth that is being defiled in efforts to unify diverse religions. [John 18:37]

Christ's first coming did not establish the Kingdom. Jesus said to Pilate, "My kingdom is not of this world. If My kingdom were of this world, My servants would fight, so that I should not be delivered to the Jews, but now My kingdom is not from here." [John 18:36] Note that He said "but *now* My kingdom is not from here." At His return, He will set up His earthly kingdom.

The Kingdom will begin with the return of the King at the end of the Tribulation and it is Israel that will receive their covenant promises in it. The Church Age remnant will share in the benefits as we return with Christ.

REVIVAL OR PERSECUTION FOR THE CHURCH?

On the lips of many is a discussion of possible revival. It sounds wonderful but we must be wary of placing our hope in human programs rather than the work of the Holy Spirit. Although global revival would be incredible, true revival historically and Biblically occurs only in small pockets, or remnants, of true believers. The Church can make the mistake of making alliances with other religions for the sake of global revival just as they compromise truth to promote world peace or global evangelism. An agenda must not be allowed to compromise the truth, regardless how well-meaning it is. It is not God's will if it is not God's way and in His timing.

Rather than a Church Age revival, there is more scriptural evidence that there will be a Tribulation revival after the Church Age ends. Even in the midst of the Tribulation, the Lord demonstrates His elegant will by balancing His wrath with great mercy. He begins by commissioning two Old Testament-style Jewish prophets to evangelize at the beginning of the Tribulation. The Lord does not leave His world devoid of salt and light for long. After the catching out of millions of Christians in the Rapture, it is a great mercy to jump-start truth in a post-Rapture world with two hand-picked preachers. One will no doubt be Elijah, either a type of that prophet or the prophet brought back to earth. [Malachi 4:5] The two witnesses preach the Gospel with an emphasis on Christ's soon return physically to the earth and accompany the Word with powerful miracles. [Revelation 11] They shed fresh truth on a deceived world.

In Revelation 7 we are introduced to one-hundred-forty-four thousand specially sealed and chosen Jewish young men from all the tribes of Israel. They are commissioned to stand for Christ under the most horrific conditions [Revelation 6:17] and witness to the truth. Their converts in the Tribulation period are "a great multitude which no one could number, of all nations, tribes, peoples, and tongues." [Revelation 7:9] This is clear evidence that Israel will be especially blessed as the evangelistic arm of the Lord in the seven years. The Lord will graft them in again and their evangelism will have tremendous results! [Romans 11:23-27]

As a final act of great mercy, God Himself will send a special envoy angel to preach the everlasting gospel from the air, possibly through the use of the airwaves or literally through a supernatural "loud voice." Our merciful Savior ensures that the Gospel is heard by every nation, tribe, tongue and people in this day of final judgment. His broadcast is simple and to the point: "Fear God and give glory to Him for the hour of His judgment has come; and worship Him who made heaven and earth, the sea and springs of water." [Revelation 14:6-7] The choice is clear: worship Satan, the destroyer, or Christ the true Creator of the universe.

It is Christ, through His chosen people Israel, that will preach truth to the entire world during the Tribulation—not the Church. Because of the great multitude that responds in faith to the Jew's evangelism, the unusual supernatural proclamation of the Lord Himself, and the fulfillment of Bible prophecy, there is strong evidence of a global revival in the time of the Tribulation. Revival is coming but not until the Church is gone.

Yes, we continue to bear witness to the truth so that those who follow Christ may escape the wrath to come. In the Great Commission we are told to assume the ongoing work of teaching, baptizing and making disciples. This work has no finish or conclusion but continues until the Church is taken out. That work is then continued by Israel—not the other way around.

Matthew 28 does not say our witness will result in global revival that will usher in the Kingdom on earth. Pockets of revival may emerge but God is not a God of quantity, but of quality.

It is not the number of conversions that glorifies Christ but the witness of His truth. He is glorified when His truth brings the lost to salvation; He is glorified when His truth is rejected. Those who are redeemed bring glory to Him for His grace and mercy; those who reject Him and are lost bring glory to Him for His holy and righteous judgment. "What if God, wanting to show His wrath and to make His power known, endured with much longsuffering the vessels of wrath prepared for destruction, and that He might make known the riches of His glory on the vessels of mercy, which He had prepared beforehand for glory, even us whom He called, not of the Jews only, but also of the Gentiles?" [Romans 9:22-24]

True believers in the Bible are relatively small in comparison with the whole; they are called remnants. Luke 13:23-24—"Then one said to Him, 'Lord, are there few who are saved?' And He said to them, 'Strive to enter through the narrow gate, for many, I say to you, will seek to enter and will not be able." Eventually the true Church will become a remnant under persecution, small in comparison to the whole. "Nevertheless, when the Son of Man comes, will He really find faith on the earth?" [Luke 18:8] It is a rhetorical question; the answer for the most part is no. "Even so then, at this present time there is a remnant according to the election of grace." [Romans 11:5] The time of the Church remnant is fast approaching in America because the Lord predicts apostasy, not revival, in the end times. [1 Timothy 4:1-5; 2 Timothy 3:1-7; Revelation 3:14-22]

The Church should be prepared for persecution, not global Christianity. Preparation spiritually, emotionally, physically and mentally is the best defense. The greatest weapon is our spiritual preparedness because nothing can defeat Christ Jesus our Lord.

Yes, things are getting worse, but our victory is coming and victory is sweet. Realistically the great divide between the lost and the redeemed should tell the discerning that a showdown is inevitable. Politicians have gone so far as to label conservative Christians terrorists. Christ said, "If the world hates you, you know that it hated Me before it hated you." [John 15:18] Expect persecution to increase in America; sisters and brothers of the faith in other cultures are already suffering and dying, some by crucifixion, starvation and beheading.

He will allow evil to fester in order to judge it at its peak because the Lord will not allow His holiness to be denigrated forever. The Lord likes to destroy evil just when it thinks it is winning...but it is His mercy that allows evil to deceive itself. His mercy is long-suffering but there is a day in which the door of the ark is shut and it is God who shuts it. He shuts the door of the Church Age first. This is the reality we are preparing for. The extent of the persecution the Church will face in America before that day is in the hands of God.

WHATEVER HAPPENED TO THE CHURCH?

The condition of America is ominously similar to Judah in the days of the prophet Isaiah. In chapter two the Lord describes why He must humble the pride and arrogance of Judah. Judah took for granted their calling as the people of God and fell into great sin; the LORD judged their pride because He alone must be exalted. [Isaiah 2:11-12] Judah was filled with eastern ways [verse 6]. So is America. We practice eastern meditation, yoga and visualization, all tools of false eastern religions to invite demonic spirits to enter our spiritual "house." Judah was "pleased with the children of foreigners" [verse 6]. So is America. We are told to tolerate foreign ways that are in conflict with Christian morality and virtue. Judah was full of silver and gold [verse 7]. So is America. Materialism has bred a generation of entitled, self-obsessed pleasure seekers. Judah was full of idols, the work of their own hands [verse 8]. So is America. We worship our own accomplishments and make idols of culture. Anything that has precedence over the worship of God becomes an idol.

Isaiah 2:12—"For the day of the LORD of hosts shall come upon everything proud and lofty, upon everything lifted up—and it shall be brought low—."

Facing the reality that persecution will increase is not an excuse to give up on America. The Great Commission instructs the Church to continue to go, make disciples, baptize, and teach while we wait for His return. [Matthew 28:18-20; Luke 19:13] This is our ongoing race, as Paul called it, until He comes. The prayers of the saints avail much; reality is a good motivator. As Americans, our primary mission field is the one in which we live.

So it is that we are seeing the beginning of the sorrows or labor pains that will precede the return of Christ. [Matthew 24:4-8] All these things will increase in frequency and intensity just as labor pains increase to bring about delivery of a child. The forecast on every front is worse and worse, not better and better. I keep making this point because it is a dividing issue in the Church and it is time to take sides. Laodicea, the last stage of the Church Age in Revelation three is described as a complacent, fence-sitting church that calls itself "Christian" while Christ is outside knocking to be allowed in [Revelation 3:14-22] and they do not realize He is absent. This last stage of the church is certainly not a picture of a victorious church that will conquer the earth for Christ.

The challenge for the remnant of true believers in the end times is to be prepared for the worst while continuing to live and work in the blessed hope of His return. We continue to pray for a spiritual awakening and continue to bear witness to the truth, but it must be done with an understanding of the times in which we live. Like Nehemiah, we keep working, but with a sword by our side and our eyes open to danger and our hope on the horizon. We are not on the Church's time table; we are on Christ's.

2 Peter 3:3-7—"...knowing this first: that scoffers will come in the last days, walking according to their own lusts, and saying, 'Where is the promise of His coming? For since the fathers fell asleep, all things continue as they were from the beginning of creation.' For this they willfully forget: that by the word of God the heavens were of old, and the earth standing out of water and in the water, by which the world that then existed perished, being flooded with water. But the heavens and the earth which are now preserved by the same word, are reserved for fire until the day of judgment and perdition of ungodly men."

Prophecy reveals this truth—conditions become much worse before they get better at His coming. Just as He judged the world with water in Noah's age, so He will judge the world by fire in the end times. [Malachi 4:1] Peace comes only after the Prince of Peace returns to enforce it. Then and only then will true hope and change be manifest in the kingdom of our Lord. The return of Christ is not a vague teaching to be ignored. It is the culmination of His eternal plan.

A FRESH PERSPECTIVE

The possibility that my generation may be the one to witness Christ's return alters my perspective spiritually. It is like looking at the planets from a long-range telescope for the first time. They are no longer just dots of light in the sky; they have form and color. I now see the Bible as His story [history] from Genesis to Revelation. He is in complete control while the world is in chaos. If He chooses not to return in my lifetime, will my enthusiasm be wasted? No, not at all. The Church was to live in such expectation from the moment He left over two thousand years ago. How can a life spent in eager anticipation of seeing Christ ever be wasted?

An expectant attitude glorifies Christ because our focus is on Him and not on us; He is the object of our faith and hope. It is like a medical doctor on call. He goes about his day at home normally, yet knowing he may be called in for an emergency at any moment. We are ready at any moment to meet Him when we hear His call. It is no wonder that those who know the King's return is imminent and invest their lives accordingly will hear "Well done good and faithful servant." [Matthew 25:23] Their lives reflect a constant state of readiness to meet their Lord in the air.

PROPHECY REVEALS THE FULLNESS OF CHRIST

Have I made the point that our perspective must be Christ-centered and not self-centered? A Christ-centered life is essential to spiritual survival. It is His Day, not ours. The last book of the Bible, the culmination of His story, affirms this absolutely because the Revelation is the full revealing of Christ in the Day of the Lord. It is all about truly knowing Him as King of Kings and Lord of Lords. The Greek word from which the English word "apocalypse" comes, an earlier title of the book, literally means "to uncover, or to reveal." (MacArthur, John. *The MacArthur Study Bible, New King James Version.* Word Publishing, 1997, p. 1992) The revealing of Christ is how the English title *Revelation* came about. We do not see the complete picture of Christ exalted until we read the rest of the story as Paul Harvey would say.

The point is this. If the Christ you worship is known only through His Gospel accounts—a gentle man walking Galilee in sandals—you do not know Christ in His fullness. Those who are ignorant of the prophetic Word have an incomplete picture of the Lord they say they love.

Christ is revealed in the Revelation as much more than our gentle, loving Jesus. As the conquering King of the world He will return wearing the uniform of a warrior high priest to seek vengeance on those who trample on His grace. [Revelation 19:11-16] He wields a sharp sword commanding justice as well as a loving God extending mercy.

Is the image of a vengeful and wrath-filled Christ disturbing? It shouldn't be. I am comforted to know He will return to judge the world. It certainly needs it. I am secure in the fact that our omnipotent, all-powerful God can destroy all our enemies in a just manner.

The Revelation mentions the wrath of God sixteen times. The Tribulation is designed to confront the idols of man and shatter them so that at Christ's return, "at the name of

Jesus every knee should bow, of those in heaven, and of those on earth, and of those under the earth, and that every tongue should confess that Jesus Christ is Lord, to the glory of God the Father." [Philippians 2:10-11]

Every creature in the universe *will* acknowledge Christ as Lord, but those who do not choose Him willingly will affirm Him in eternal hell. Only the remnant of true believers from every people, tongue and nation will be saved. When Christ returns He will establish His kingdom on earth and reign on the throne of David for one thousand years and we will be with Him. [Revelation 19-20]

Although world conditions will continue to worsen and chaos will increase, remember the prophetic map we have been given to follow. Look for shadows of God's sovereign hand on history. God's creation is not out of control even in the midst of social chaos. He is orchestrating everything.

THE WORD IS A LIGHT UNTO MY PATH

2 Peter 1:19—"And so we have the prophetic word confirmed, which you do well to heed as a light that shines in a dark place, until the day dawns and the morning star rises in your hearts."

Until Christ our morning star appears for the Church, prophecy shines a bright light on the unknown. We can walk into a dark room without fear as long as we know what is there. Even if the electricity goes out, we are able to find our way around our own home in the dark. If we are lost in an unknown place without light, however, fear is understandable. But the future is not an unknown. We need not fear because Christ wins! After the Rapture we will have a front row seat in heaven better than the fifty yard line to witness His victory.

~

Practical Prepping

Herbs and seasonings make anything tasty, even canned goods. Add fresh or dried basil to canned spaghetti sauce to enhance the tomatoes; basil and tomatoes always go together. Then add marjoram or oregano for an authentic Italian taste, and a bit of dried chili pepper for a "kick." If you like a sweeter sauce, add brown sugar to taste. Herbs replace the fresh flavor cooked out in the canning process.

Culinary herbs always have a place in my garden: oregano or marjoram for Italian, onion chives, garlic chives, French tarragon for chicken and fish, sweet basil for tomatoes, cilantro/coriander seed for salsa and Asian cooking, dill for pickling, mints for tea, and rosemary or English thyme for meats. I use them fresh all summer and then collect enough to dry and use all winter. This is an economical way to stock the kitchen. If you do not cook with herbs, begin to experiment. Herbs make even rice and beans savory.

~

7

BUILDING YOUR SPIRITUAL BOMB SHELTER

"I will love You, O LORD, my strength.

The LORD is my rock and my fortress and my deliverer;

My God, my strength, in whom I will trust;

My shield and the horn of my salvation, my stronghold.

I will call upon the LORD, who is worthy to be praised;

So shall I be saved from my enemies."

Psalm 18:1-3

~

THE LORD IS OUR STRONGHOLD

Building a spiritual bomb shelter is not as easy as downloading blueprints from the internet. It is not natural—it is supernatural. It is also not hype like "Take this pill and lose thirty pounds in thirty days." There is no magic bullet in spiritual hope and faith.

But the good news is that the results are just as tangible as and much more effective than a magic mantra. Like everything else worth attaining, it requires effort—spiritual effort. God designed it that way so that He alone receives the glory; if it were easy, we would not value it.

Let me state it like this: The Lord is as much of a fortress and stronghold in our life as we allow Him to be, or as we believe Him to be. God does His best work when we can do nothing. This is not to say we are to sit back and let God do all the work; but when we are in a position where we cannot contribute, we truly see His power on display because it is none of us.

It comes down to control. Is God in control of our lives or are we steering more than we should? For women especially, control is often about fear—fear of giving God control of something we are afraid to live without. The irony is that if we do give Him complete access—complete control of that which we fear losing—the only thing we truly lose is the fear.

Allowing Him sovereign control means we allow Him to work in and through us instead of our taking the lead. No, it is not a free ride. Like a tandem bike, we are peddling; but He is doing the steering. Much of our spiritual training involves learning to let God work through us instead of our operating in our own strength. We accomplish great things by faith when it is not our human might or power, but by His Spirit. [Zechariah 4:6] Only then are we abiding in Him and He in us.

This spiritual submission is not weakness; just the opposite. It is the spiritual attitude that allows God to work great strength in us. "Blessed are the meek, for they shall inherit the earth." [Matthew 5:5]

A few years ago I passed through a dark valley. It was not the first time in my life. Trials are allowed for a reason. I thank my Lord for every one of them but they are not pleasant. It hurts to be polished into fine gold. This particular trial was to break the stranglehold of a fear that gripped my life. I didn't even know to what extent I was in bondage, but He did. Laying down a pet fear meant I had to give control completely to God and not take it back.

In order to expose my fear He allowed a perfect storm of threatened loss. I slipped into a state of anxiety. In order to sleep, I prayed the twenty-third Psalm, walking through the passage as if Christ were leading me to green pastures and still waters. His peace transcended my fear and became a very real comfort.

Dark valleys are a part of life; knowing Christ is the light at the end of the tunnel is the only sure deliverance. Christ our good Shepherd has in His strong arms two tools: a rod to fight our enemies and a crooked staff to pull us through. When we trust in Him, we need not fear. Even when the darkness falls, our Shepherd can bring us through.

Paul said it like this: *"Who shall separate us from the love of Christ? Shall tribulation, or distress, or persecution, or famine, or nakedness, or peril, or sword?... Yet in all these things we are more than conquerors through Him who loved us. For I am persuaded that neither death nor life, nor angels nor principalities nor powers, nor things present nor things to come, nor height nor depth, nor any other created thing, shall be able to separate us from the love of God which is in Christ Jesus our Lord." [Romans 8:35-39]*

Do we truly know that all things work together for good to those who love God and are the called according to His purpose? [Romans 8:28] If we truly believe that, we should be able to let go of anything knowing He has our best interests at heart. Unfortunately, we often must learn the hard way. He brought me through that valley and slayed another fear that was making my faith weak. I am much better for it and praise His name.

FAITH INTO SHOE LEATHER

How do we translate spiritual faith into practical shoe leather? The answer is not the one we want. Faith becomes real by testing. It is not human nature to naturally trust in invisible things and future hopes. In order to turn faith into tangible reality, we must live supernaturally, not naturally. The only way to learn how to do that is to experience faith that goes beyond the flesh. Test it and know that it is real.

"Lord, I believe; help my unbelief!" [Mark 9:24] This was the prayer of the desperate father of the demon-possessed boy. He asked the disciples to heal his son while Christ was on the Mount of Transfiguration with Peter, James and John. The disciples waiting at the foot of the mount could not do it. Why couldn't they heal this boy when they were able to cast out demons and heal earlier? [Mark 6:13]

The Spirit operates only in obedience to the Trinity; in this instance the power to heal was not given to them because Christ intended to use the incident to heal more than the boy; He wanted to demonstrate how weak faith becomes strong faith—through testing. The son had been tortured by the demon since his childhood. We might excuse the father's tentative "If you can do anything…" after years of severe trial and the failed attempt by the other disciples. But Christ did not excuse his lack of faith. He demanded more of the father—more faith. In order to engender it in him, he drove out the vicious demon spirit. Christ answered the father's greater prayer and healed the father's unbelief. The power of faith is in Christ, according to His sovereign control, and for His glory.

New products are put through rigorous tests and trials in order to prove they deliver what they promise. When a product wins the Good Housekeeping Seal of Approval, housewives trust it. When we come through the fire and our spiritual armor protects us, we learn to trust that armor. When Christ answers prayer, our faith grows.

Paul assures the believer that true faith gives us access to "peace with God through our Lord Jesus Christ." Even in the midst of war, we can live in spiritual peace that transcends our circumstances. "And not only that, but we also glory in tribulations, knowing that tribulation produces perseverance, and perseverance, character; and character, hope. Now hope does not disappoint, because the love of God has been poured out in our hearts by the Holy Spirit who was given to us." [Romans 5:1-5]

Reading Paul's words, I'm almost tempted to ask the Lord for another trial in order to strengthen my hope. But the Lord doesn't require us to volunteer; we are all subject to trials and suffering. Much of it is a consequence of a fallen world; God works it for good. Much of it is a result of our own acts of sin; God works it for good. Much of it is allowed by God in order to build our faith. "And we know that all things work together for good to those who love God, to those who are the called according to His purpose." [Romans 8:28-29]. It is extremely comforting to know that whatever we go through, if we keep our eyes on a loving Savior and submit to His purpose, it will all work out for good. One event in our lives brought this truth into vivid reality to the Clemens family.

A PERSONAL STORY OF FAITH BUILDING

My husband and I and our children lived through over thirteen years of testing that resulted in spiritual wisdom and faith equivalent to an Ivy League education. We learned to live by faith the hard way. At times our faith was tested to the point where we virtually walked on water to survive. One day in particular summarized our journey.

It was not the best day for a hike. Recent rains made the trail muddy and a chill wind reminded us it was early spring of 1983. We did not choose the day for the weather. It was the only available time we had to fulfill our son's merit badge requirement—an hour's hike with the family.

The deep recession of the eighties took longer to reach "the pocket of prosperity" of Central Illinois, but when it did, it hit like a bomb shell. Several large employers either shut their doors or pulled out for new locations with lower manufacturing and labor costs. One of the companies that relocated was my husband's. We made the decision not to move south with them thinking with his education and experience, he could find another job near our home. After a year and a half of searching, we faced the fact that a management degree would not provide a job in a severe recession economy. My husband began retraining in IT at the local junior college.

We watched our savings slowly melt away after weeks and months, helpless to do anything about it. All of our resources were applied to meeting mortgage payments and necessities. We learned to be content with a limited lifestyle and spent a lot of time walking, talking and praying together. Through a convergence of opportunities, the Lord eventually led us to consider starting our own business. He began opening doors and we went through them.

Our leading was to open a retail shop and small restaurant in an old barn on my parents' property near our home. We rented the building and obtained a loan to put our own money into the renovation. It took a lot of sweat equity and creativity but we began to turn a one hundred year old shell of a dairy barn into shops and a tea room. In order to open before the holiday season, we worked ten and twelve hour days, a commitment that left little time for entertainment.

It was an overcast Saturday that found us driving to a wooded area park to steal a few hours of relaxation as a family. After a light sack lunch on the trail, our son Dirk led us to follow the yellow arrows through the dense undergrowth. Our first obstacle was crossing a stream swollen by spring rains; the stepping stones were covered by rushing water. The four of us dutifully removed shoes and socks and waded over carefully. After replacing our moist footwear, we moved on through the grass and weeds infiltrating the trail.

The winding path looped back bringing us to another crossing of the same stream. This time we were less careful removing shoes and socks. When the trail doubled back a third time, we plunged in shoes and all.

The short trek we planned became much longer as the trail took us in circles. Although the park was only a few miles from our home, we were unfamiliar with it and unprepared to find such a heavily wooded hiking trail. We didn't bother to find a map thinking surely the trails wouldn't be very demanding. We were wrong. Going up and down the ravines and crossing the stream several times took a toll on my husband who is diabetic. He quickly burned the carbs he had eaten for lunch and had too much insulin left in his system. He sat down on the trail experiencing an insulin reaction, his blood sugar too low to go on. I didn't know what I would do if he passed out as we didn't know exactly where we were. We had no food left, except for some small candy jaw breakers our son had in his pocket, under his wet socks. My husband wiped them off as best he could and ate them and began to revive.

At this point we had to make a decision—do we turn back or go forward? We knew we had a tough hike going back. Surely it couldn't be that far to the parking lot. As a family, we decided to go on. I remember praying and feeling so frustrated and lost, yet walking blindly forward. Our children were ages six and eight at the time but they walked on their own and forged ahead. To them, it was a kind of adventure and it was better that way.

The trail led to a knob planted with fir trees. I was awed to find myself in whispering pines hung with brightly colored bird houses, courtesy of a local Scout troop. It was surreal encountering a haven of color in the midst of overgrown woods. The breeze was sighing and the birds were singing in this small island of calm, oblivious to the strange situation in which we found ourselves. It was a welcome glimpse of civilization as we had spotted no other living soul the whole time we were on the trail.

The stream came across our path again; we sloshed through it. Our little band was looking quite bedraggled. The trail broke out onto a back road. I suddenly knew where we were. For a crazy moment I thought we should just walk home but it was at least seven miles and we had walked miles already. These were the days before cell phones and I have come to truly appreciate their convenience. I thought about finding a house down the road and calling someone to pick us up, but we thought that sounded too much like giving up—too desperate. I have often wondered about the wisdom of that decision; but at the time, going on seemed to be where the Lord was leading.

The road led down into a valley where the trail continued; Dirk found another arrow and raced up the hill followed closely by his dad. Kelly and I trudged behind them. We passed the ruined foundation of an old farm house surrounded by tangles of broken fencing and barbed wire covered with weeds. Someone had lived there but now it was gone; everything they had worked for was ruined. I wondered if our hard work would produce something lasting in the competitive retail world or would we see our dreams lost?

The trail led to an open field filled with broken corn stalks. It had not yet been plowed to ready it for planting. Why would a corn field be in the boundaries of the park, with the trail leading around it? We stood in the center wondering which direction to go. Kelly and her dad saw something on a distant fence post that might be a marker. It looked so far away. I wanted to make sure before walking another step feeling over-whelmed. They motioned to us and we began to follow slowly.

Dirk and I cut across and passed a small grave yard on the edge of the field filled with weathered sandstone markers. I had done research on the history of the area and didn't know this grave yard existed. For a moment I forgot about our situation and walked into the shadows to see if I could find a date on one of the stones. Most of the information was worn away. Dense trees surrounded the shadowed cluster of stones blocking the wind and the light. I suddenly realized how quiet and eerie it was as if I was transported to another place. What was I doing in a grave yard when I should be following my family and getting home? I turned quickly to see my young son waiting at the entrance for me; I was glad he was there. I would often be glad of his presence in the years ahead. We walked quickly to catch up with my husband and daughter.

The trail was taking us back into the denseness along Kickapoo Creek. Now we began trudging quietly, just trying to keep going. The planned hour-long hike had turned into several hours and we didn't know how much longer it would take to find the trail head. We were encouraged to see another couple coming down the trail from the opposite direction dressed in hiking gear. I almost asked them how far to the parking lot but they looked at us so strangely, I didn't. We did look a sight—tired, muddy, and windblown, like something out of The Grapes of Wrath. We knew now something must be ahead, but the hill was the steepest we had yet to climb, and slippery.

We climbed almost on our knees. I was so tired after weeks of hard work and emotional stress I didn't think I was going to make it unless it was on my knees. If my husband was having any further trouble, he wasn't telling me. It was at this moment as we were all struggling that my husband came up with a brilliant idea. He announced, "When we get back to the car, we are going to Dairy Queen and you can have anything you want!"

Because of our tight budget, treats had been rare for the last two years. My husband began to chant "D.Q., D.Q., D.Q.," and the kids chimed in. In my fatigue I began to laugh giddily which made it even harder to climb. When we got to the top, there was the parking lot. Our car never looked so good. Silently, we piled in.

My husband drove immediately to the Dairy Queen in the nearest town. He and Dirk both ordered banana splits. I ate an entire Peanut Buster Parfait, and Kelly asked for what she always got at Dairy Queen—a chocolate dipped cone. After gorging on ice cream we drove home and collapsed in the living room. All the work we had planned for that Saturday was not going to get done. We slept away the rest of the afternoon. As we told our story to friends, we were informed that the trail we took is fifteen miles long and snakes through the entire park acreage.

I asked the Lord what that quirky incident had been all about. He knew we had been running on little but adrenalin. Why had He allowed us to lose a whole day and push us to our limits? He didn't answer me at that time. It would be nearly ten years before I received my answer. If He had told me that the hike was a parable of what we were about to face in our business, I don't know if I could have gone on.

We have been asked what it is like starting a business with little but hope, an idea, and a banker who takes a risk. I tell them it is the hardest work you will ever do but what you learn as a family is worth more than a Harvard education. My husband and I and our two children worked together; we couldn't have done it without the kids and their support. Kelly began bussing tables when she was eight, her long hair in a pigtail and the apron dragging around her ankles. Dirk worked in the gardens and helped his dad with maintenance until he was old enough to wash dishes. He quickly realized he enjoyed cooking more than dish washing and eventually trained as a prep cook. He became one of our best cooks and still cooks for he and his wife Julie today. Kelly graduated to server and eventually grew into her apron. They both were employed by our business all through high school and many summers during college earning their own expense money.

Our children were considered co-owners of our business and learned marketing, restaurant management, the wholesale/retail market, the secondary market shopping antique and collectible venues, and how to work with employees and the public. The experience they gained proved to be extremely beneficial as they made their own way into the professional work force after college. They acquired Christian management principles from their dad and marketing and creativity from their mom.

It wasn't easy not being able to provide the best for our children when jobs were non-existent and the savings were gone but it gave us more appreciation for what we did have. In return, the Lord provided what was more important—a good work ethic, the accomplishment of being part of something special, a wealth of first-hand experience, an impressive resume' and the undisputable evidence that faith and prayer work. In those years of demanding labor and sacrifice, there was no opportunity for an entitlement mentality to take root.

Owning and operating retail and collectable shops and a restaurant also taught my husband and me many invaluable lessons. I began to find an outlet for the creative gifts and talents God has given me and proudly watched my husband skillfully handle the administrative parts of the business. We both have our own strengths and they worked beautifully together. Our business, The Farm Grove Shops and Restaurant, was blessed with popularity and a good reputation. Customers became friends and Bible study partners.

THE PARABLE OF THE HIKE

The meaning of our accidental fifteen mile hike would become clear years later. It is a parable of trials and overcoming that is common to all of us. There were days of bright-colored bird houses in pine-scented trees during our Farm Grove adventure when business was good and our special events were a celebration. But there were other times when business was slow and issues with my extended family took the joy out of what we were doing. The same conflicts stemming from control issues in my childhood returned again and again, like that pesky stream that kept cropping up to make our life cold and miserable. Why do we have to cross it again? I wanted to run away and hide but our investment committed us to forge ahead on the path and keep going. It also forced me to confront the affects of emotional abuse rather than run away from it.

At times the oppression was so great it was like operating in the deadness of a grave yard. I often cried out to the Lord to tell us which way to go. The people who were supposed to love me were the ones making it hardest for us to survive. At those times the Lord sent intercessors to pray, often in a miraculous way, and our son and daughter were always there with us. My husband stood against the injustices we faced as a buffer, swallowing his pride and often allowing others to take credit for his hard work in order to keep peace.

One of the blessings to come from it was learning to pray together as a couple, often on our knees. I am humbled that it took a trial to teach us this precious tool. We prayed that the Lord would heal the broken relationships and take care of the injustice. Eventually He did just that. We discovered the power of prayer between a Christian husband and wife. If I had been able to run from the hurt, I would have forsaken family ties completely and probably would never have gotten over it.

Instead necessity tied us to the conflict so that we had to confront it by faith. That was God's plan. He took His resolution for my husband's job loss and used it to heal deep-seated pain. But He did so by walking us through the fire to get to the other side.

I am still learning patience even after He has allowed me to plunge into the same cold water many times; but I am improving, letting patience have its perfect work, that I can be perfect and complete, lacking nothing. When I am in a graveyard of darkness or anxiety, I know I am never alone when He is with me. The presence of family and my Lord is so much more precious now and always will be.

As we look back on the full twenty-six years in which we operated a business, I would not trade our experiences for anything. The Lord used it as a catalyst to bring hurts to the surface, cauterize them and heal them. The Lord blessed us with abundant spiritual blessings that are sweeter than ice cream. It is a bittersweet reality that faith is grown in trials and suffering. We obtain it the hard way. Our children witnessed our faith walk first-hand and learned to apply it to their own lives. You cannot buy that kind of education.

Our road ahead was unseen, although He gave us a living sketch we would understand later. As His Word says, all things do work together for good to those who love Him and are the called who submit to His purpose [Romans 8:28]. That truth has become living faith in our lives, no matter what the trial.

THANK HIM

In Proverbs we are told to acknowledge Him in all our ways—in whatever we are doing [Proverbs 3:5]. In suffering, I am learning to acknowledge Him *during* the suffering by thanking Him ahead of time for the good that will come out of it [Romans 8:28], even when I don't feel like it. That simple act of obedience often changes my feelings.

James 1:2-4—"My brethren, count it all joy when you fall into various trials, knowing that the testing of your faith produces patience. But let patience have its perfect work, that you may be perfect and complete, lacking nothing."

SUFFERING ENDS

We could not see the end of the trail, but we knew it had to be ahead. The problem was that we didn't know if we had the strength to make it. But we did, through His strength.

1 Peter 5:6-7, 10-11—"Therefore humble yourselves under the mighty hand of God, that He may exalt you in due time, casting all your care upon Him, for He cares for you... But may the God of all grace, who called us to His eternal glory by Christ Jesus, after you have suffered a while, perfect, establish, strengthen, and settle you. To Him be the glory and the dominion forever and ever. Amen."

Know this about suffering; it ends. The promise of Christ is that when it ends, we are better for having suffered. If there is some bitterness and anger in your life regarding loss or pain, cast this care on Christ and let Him show you the supernatural good that can come out of it. Our attitude concerning trials is what separates us from unbelievers because praising Him for suffering is not natural—it is supernatural. Do we truly believe that Christ is perfecting, establishing, strengthening and settling us to make us better than we were before? When we do, we are *living* faith.

We may walk through the valley of the shadow of death but in Christ there is light at the end of the tunnel. [Psalm 23]

~

Practical Prepping

Every family has a keeper—someone who keeps everything, and not just family mementoes. They may keep bread wrappers, twist ties, take-out boxes, cottage cheese containers, used ribbon and wrapping paper, aluminum foil and foil containers, and jars of every sort and size. I used to think only depression era people did this; then recycling made it more popular. I now keep a lot of what used to go in the trash for purely frugal reasons.

Why use a paper towel for vegetable peelings when the newspaper does a better job? Even if the juice soaks through, a few layers of newspaper do not tear easily. I keep a nice stack of sections under the shelf in the panty to pull out when I need some; the rest of the paper is stacked downstairs to use for kindling in our fire pit. Then there are those rubber bands around the newspaper which I use for everything, including hanging herbs. At times I send leftovers or dessert home with the family in disposable containers I have saved from restaurants. Tupper Ware that leaves the house may never find its way home.

We are not on a public sewer system and do not have a garbage disposal. Those cottage cheese containers are excellent for throwing away things like the greasy broth from the crock pot. The sturdy ones can be used for freezing fruit. If you have ripe fruit such as apples, berries or peaches that you cannot eat fast enough, stir some sugar into the peeled and sliced fruit, pour into your container, use black marker to label it with the date and contents, and put it in the freezer. The next time you need pie filling or a side dish for dinner put it in the refrigerator to unthaw. Frozen fruit is excellent for quick smoothies.

~

8

WAITING-WATCHING-WORKING

WAITING-WATCHING

The Church has lost something our Lord cares about deeply—the desire to wait and watch expectantly for His return. We wait expectantly for the birth of a child, we wait expectantly for a summer vacation, we wait expectantly for the first blossoms of spring and the turning leaves of fall. But we have lost the excitement of waiting and watching expectantly for the return of Christ. The last prayer of the Bible is "Even so, come, Lord Jesus!" [Revelation 22:20] John's emotional prayer should be our own.

John had just witnessed, through supernatural time travel, all the glory and horror of the tribulation; and yet he prayed that Jesus would come. That is the motivation that can be ours, even if we suffer persecution, even if we go through painful trials, even if we lose our material comforts, we know Christ is coming. Christ desires that His bride, His Church, lives in constant expectation of the wedding feast and cannot wait to set eyes on her Bridegroom. He often used parables to illustrate that not only *should* we be waiting and watching; He expects it.

- Matthew 24:42-44 – "Watch therefore, for you do not know what hour your Lord is coming. But know this, that if the master of the house had known what hour the thief would come, he would have watched and not allowed his house to be broken into. Therefore you also be ready, for the Son of Man is coming at an hour you do not expect." Just as a homeowner would take measures to protect the house from burglars if he knew they were coming, so Christ expects us to be fully prepared to go out and meet Him when He returns. Although the Church knows the general signs of His coming and the Tribulation Saints will be counting down the actual events of the seven years, neither remnant will know the exact hour when He will break through the clouds. [Matthew 25:13] None-the-less, we are to be constantly watching.

- Mark 13:32-36; Mark 13:32-37 – "...And what I say to you, I say to all: Watch!"
- Luke 21:34-36 –" Watch therefore, and pray always that you may be counted worthy to escape all these things that will come to pass, and to stand before the Son of Man." Prophecy is not essential to salvation; however, it has a lot to say about how worthily the bride has deported herself in His absence.
- Matthew 26:38, 40-41 – The night of His arrest, our Lord longed to have His disciples awake and watching with Him—but they slept. So He longs that we are awake and watching for His return.
- 1 Corinthians 16:13-14 – "Watch, stand fast in the faith, be brave, be strong. Let all that you do be done with love."
- 2 Timothy 4:1-5 – "...But you be watchful in all things, endure afflictions, do the work of an evangelist, fulfill your ministry."

1 Peter 4:7-11 – The passage outlined below from Peter contains practical information as to how to live the Christian life in the end times. Notice that his words are directed *to* believers *for* service to other believers first.

- Be serious and watchful in your prayers knowing the end of all things is at hand.
- Have fervent love for other believers. Love begins in the Church and our first responsibility is to brothers and sisters in Christ. This will have more significance as persecution increases and the Church may have to go underground in remnant groups to support each other.
- Be hospitable to one another without grumbling. The Acts Church had all things in common. This was not socialism; it means they met the needs of those less prepared as they would members of their immediate family. If a brother or sister in Christ comes to our door in need, we are to welcome them.
- We are to administer our spiritual gifts for the benefit of other believers. As mentioned under WORKING in the section following, if we are to administer our gifts with zeal, we must know what they are. Ask the Lord for spiritual discernment to discover your strengths; He will answer.
- Above all, do all things that God may be glorified. *The answer to every question is to bring God glory*. Why does God allow suffering? To bring God glory. Why is He coming again? To bring God glory. It is all about Him; but our joy comes as a result. We are to trust in Christ alone through His Spirit. In John 15:5 He said that without Him we can do nothing. When Christ is responsible for the outcome, He rightly receives the glory.

If I had to choose one passage that summarizes the importance of fervent waiting and watching, it would be:

1 Thessalonians 5:5-11 – "You are all sons of light and sons of the day. We are not of the night nor of darkness. Therefore let us not sleep, as others do, but let us watch and be sober. For those who sleep, sleep at night, and those who get drunk are drunk at night. But let us who are of the day be sober, putting on the breastplate of faith and love, and as a helmet the hope of salvation. For God did not appoint us to wrath, but to obtain salvation through our Lord Jesus Christ, who died for us, that whether we wake or sleep, we should live together with Him. Therefore comfort each other and edify one another, just as you also are doing."

There is nothing worse than flying blind. In Daniel chapter twelve, Daniel was told that only those who are wise concerning Christ will understand what is happening in the time of the end. This passage contains all the points I have tried to emphasize. There are those in the Church who are awake to what God is doing and there are those who are asleep. Those who are awake are of the day. Christ is the light of the world and gives us spiritual discernment from His Word. There is no excuse for a believer to be complacent, uninformed or asleep. If I could pick a slogan for a T-shirt it would be *Wide Awake and Lookin' Up!* Those with spiritual discernment would know what it meant.

The believer lives in expectation of His any-moment return but it is sober, serious expectation. We arm ourselves for battle with a breastplate of *faith* and love and a helmet of the *hope* of salvation and deliverance. We are wide awake to the challenges that may precede His wrath but God did not appoint us to the wrath of the Tribulation.

Therefore the Church has *comfort* which no other segment of society can have. The Church is to share that comfort with other believers. We are not waiting for the appearance of Antichrist—we are waiting for Christ Jesus to catch out the Church.

WORKING

Patience may be a virtue but it is spiritual fruit I continue to work on. Anything that involved standing in line was torture before I was a believer but the Holy Spirit can sanctify even a bad attitude. I remember a Christian children's record the kids played—a turtle singing about having patience. It was a cute little song that ended "Have patience...and think of all the times when others had to wait for you!" I began to do that. Now I plan meals, mentally go through my prayer list, or calmly day dream while standing in line. If I am irritated with someone holding up the line in front of me, I pray for them. I have no idea what their circumstances are. The situation may have been the Lord's way of bringing their prayer needs to someone's attention. It is certainly His way of bringing my attitude to my attention.

I am well aware that until I gain total victory over impatience, He will continue to put me in long check-out lanes where a problem invariably arises just to test me. He is not vindictive in this; He wants me to be the best Sharon I can be. What does patience have to do with working while we wait? Everything. Those who wait impatiently can fall into the trap of setting dates or giving up on His return completely. That is when our working can become centered on our agenda rather than His.

Waiting can especially be torture if we are waiting for the other shoe to drop in evil times. Time goes faster when we are occupied in meaningful work. "See then that you walk circumspectly, not as fools but as wise, redeeming the time, because the days are evil." [Ephesians 5:15-16]

YOUR SPECIAL CALLING

How do we redeem the time with meaningful work? This is where I talk about the specific calling each of us has in Christ so that we can be actively involved while we wait expectantly for Him. We exist to bring Him glory. "He has decreed for His own glory all things that come to pass." [Ephesians 1:11] But we also have a particular job description hand-picked for us. Performing our Christ-appointed tasks is what brings Him glory. "For we are His workmanship, created in Christ Jesus for good works, which God prepared beforehand that we should walk in them." [Ephesians 2:10]

Did you know that you were created with a destiny, a particular job description? Fulfilling His calling for us is how we occupy until He comes and glorify Him to the best of our ability. We are a puzzle piece in His grand scheme of things and no other person can complete the big picture.

The feedback I hear when I tell groups that we exist for a particular reason is that most don't think they have any particular skills, gifts or talents that God can use. Women especially wrongly believe this because they compare themselves to others instead of asking the Master what He intended for them. The Architect of the human race doesn't make inferior products. Each of us has at least one spiritual gift or a combination of gifts. [1 Corinthians 12:7] Combined with personality, strengths and talents, each believer is unique.

"I will praise You, for I am fearfully and wonderfully made; marvelous are Your works, and that my soul knows very

117

well. My frame was not hidden from You when I was made in secret, and skillfully wrought in the lowest parts of the earth. Your eyes saw my substance, being yet unformed. And in Your book they all were written, the days fashioned for me, when as yet there were none of them." [Psalm 139:14-16]

I can only speak from personal experience as to how to discover what the Lord designed each of us to do. First, I asked Him. Then, I tried some areas of work in the Church and quickly found out what I enjoyed and what I did not and what He shut the door on. The Lord has designed us for fullness of joy in Him, not drudgery [John 15:11]. If we are not good with kids, are we the best candidate for the junior high department? If we are not called to the mission field in some far-off place, should we still go out of guilt or miss-placed duty? We would be a poor missionary if we were supposed to be fulfilling God's purpose doing something else—somewhere else.

I also took a spiritual gifts test to affirm what I really already knew—that my greatest joy and assurance of God's empowerment was in teaching. I have some leaning in other areas but teaching is dominant. In fact my gifts are very limited in that teaching far outweighs everything else. That is not necessarily the best because it makes my ability in Christ somewhat narrow.

Please understand. I have served doing other things besides teaching: VBS crafts, taking care of children, working in the kitchen, picking up trash, stuffing envelopes and serving on a prayer team. When there is a need, I try to fill it. However the Church operates the most efficiently when a foot doesn't try to be a hand; the results could be an inefficient hand and a leg without a foot.

By far the best way to discover what you were created to do is to look for what you enjoy doing and have success in. I enjoy studying, reading God's Word, discussing spiritual topics and teaching what I have learned. When a truth is illuminated in His Word, I cannot wait to share it with someone. The Lord affirmed this gift by opening doors for me to teach again and again.

Even in the area of teaching, He would at times close the door in order to guide me to other teaching options or to make sure I was not usurping His authority and trying to go it alone. I now write a Christian newsletter, mentor young women who want to study the Word, and lead Bible studies. I also write Christian fiction and non-fiction. The result is a life that brings me joy and complete fulfillment with the peace of knowing I am living in His will for me.

When you find your area of spiritual fulfillment, put everything you have into it. "Whatever your hand finds to do, do it with your might; for there is no work or device or knowledge or wisdom in the grave where you are going." [Ecclesiastes 9:10] Hard work and enthusiasm is the Christian calling for everything we do. Imagine what results when our hard work meets His spiritual destiny.

WORK WHILE IT IS YET DAY

There is an element of urgency in finding our spiritual job description. Christ knew His time was short before He went to the cross. "I must work the works of Him who sent Me while it is day; the night is coming when no one can work." [John 9:4] The time before the Rapture when the door of the Church age closes may also be short. Even if He does not come to catch out the Church in our lifetime, we should seek urgently the particular work He has for us to do here and now. The trick is to be already-ready. Whatever particular specialty is ours in the work of the Church, we are all to witness to the truth by telling others about Christ. The most effective way of doing that is within the arena of specialty He places us. The Lord is calling together the remnant of the Church and we have an opportunity to be His vehicle of truth while we are still here.

WORK EXPECTANTLY

The Word is clear that although we live in expectation of His coming, we are not to neglect our predestined duties. Anticipation and work go together; expectation doesn't mean sitting in the porch swing all day. If you have not yet discovered what your spiritual work is, it is time.

Luke 12:35-37a—"Let your waist be girded and your lamps burning; and you yourselves be like men who wait for their master, when he will return from the wedding, that when he comes and knocks they may open to him immediately. Blessed are those servants whom the master, when he comes, will find watching."

In the parable of the ten minas the Lord likened Himself to a nobleman who went into a far country to receive a kingdom and to return. Does this sound familiar? He told his servants, "Do business till I come." We are to occupy until He comes, maintaining our Christian watch while working and waiting. How we occupy or how we do the business of the Lord is between Him and us. I do not believe any two jobs are exactly the same because God is too creative to copy Himself. Part of our hope at His return is hearing "Well done, good servant..." [Luke 19:11-27] That is what we strive for when we stand before Him at the Rapture. Works do not save us; they are the evidence that we are saved because Christ is in us in the person of the Holy Spirit and we are a new creature [2 Corinthians 5:17]. We cannot help but produce spiritual fruit if we are operating as a new creature.

We should be motivated to work for Him not only because it is our spiritual nature to do what we were designed to do and bring Him glory; we are also motivated because He promises rewards to good servants. It may be news to some believers that right after the Lord catches out the Church we go through a rewards ceremony called the Bema or The Judgment Seat of Christ. It is not a judgment of salvation; no one is caught out who is not already saved in Christ; works do not save. It is a judgment to determine rewards for what we did while in the body. The scriptures are as follows:

- 1 Corinthians 3:10-15 – The "Day" that will declare whether we produced something precious and lasting or just kindling is the Day of Christ, the Rapture. That Day is not to be confused with the Day of the Lord which is the Tribulation and return of Christ. [Zephaniah 1:14, 15] The Day of Christ is also in Philippians 1:10.
- 1 Corinthians 4:5
- 2 Corinthians 5:9-10
- Philippians 1:9-11
- 1 Peter 1:7
- Romans 14:10-13

As in the parables of the talents and the minas, the Lord determines what responsibility we will have during the earthly kingdom and in eternity from this Bema meeting. "Then each one's praise will come from God." [1 Corinthians 4:5] Our reward may be represented in a tangible type of crown but it becomes our joy to be able to cast our crowns before the throne at the feet of Christ. [Revelation 4:9-11] It is our reward but it is done for His glory.

Only work accomplished for His glory, with His strength, in His time and for His purpose will pass the test. What we do for our own glory in our own way will not. The Word says we will suffer loss when self-styled work is burned up. [1 Corinthians 3:15] It is my thought that although we are overjoyed to be with Him in heaven, the loss may involve knowing we could have done more for our Savior when we had the opportunity. He is the Bridegroom of the Bride. We want to present ourselves as a beautiful bride, adorned with gold and jewels of self-less service. Some may stand before Him clothed only in the white robes of righteousness because of His salvation...and smelling like smoke.

Although I do not choose to be a martyr, I believe His grace will be with me if persecution increases and that is my destiny. If my destiny is not martyrdom and I am raptured, when I look into His eyes of love and purity, I believe I will be sorry I did not die for the one who died for me. That would be suffering loss.

~

Practical Prepping

Surreal Moments

Glimpses of God's smile arrived as unexpected gifts during the hard work and long hours of our retail/restaurant business. I recall vividly one summer evening after dinner. I found my family outside looking at the ripe wheat field across the road. The sun was going down in the west and casting pink light onto the golden grain, turning it into a surreal swath of rose gold. The color was fantastic. And then, as if He said "You haven't seen anything yet," the fireflies turned on their iridescent tail lights.

We have yet to see so many fireflies in one place, hovering in blinking array over the pink field. The four of us stood, staring, knowing that this incredible scene would last only as long as the sun perched on the horizon behind us. It is a memory we call Fireflies in the Wheat Field. I wish I were an artist at times like that but I doubt anyone could have done it justice. He is the Master.

~

9

OCCUPY UNTIL HE COMES

"Your mission, should you choose to accept it…" The 1966 TV series Mission Impossible began each episode with those challenging words. We have all been given a mission—to be busy with His work while we wait and watch, until He takes us out in the Rapture or we die and are resurrected at the Rapture.

This waiting/working/watching attitude will separate those prepared for His any-moment return from those who are complacent. The faith and hope the remnant has in the Lord's return will equip the Church for whatever trials we must go through before He appears in the clouds to take us home.

- In chapter one, THE SECRET OF SURVIVAL, I made the case that *faith* and *hope* will sustain us through any trial, including the transition period until the Rapture. We are to perfect a *living faith* that is as tangible as walking on water. We are to take comfort in a *living hope* based on the promised deliverance of the Church into the arms of Christ.
- In chapter two, THE RAPTURE/RESURRECTION OF THE CHURCH, I took you through the Biblical description of the Day of Christ, the blessed hope of the Church.
- In chapter three, THE PRETRIBULATION RAPTURE, I made the Biblical case for the Rapture event occurring before the Tribulation. The Church is not appointed to wrath.

- In chapter four, SHADOWS OF THE FOUR HORSEMEN OF THE APACALYPSE, I presented the case that prophetic signs of the times are pointing to the soon return of Christ.
- In chapter five, STORM CLOUDS ON THE HORIZON, I shared that this book is from the point-of-view of a baby boomer who has witnessed the world becoming worse and worse. My eyes were opened when I understood the blessed hope of Christ's return through His prophetic Word.
- In chapter six, HIS SOVEREIGN PURPOSE, I shared that a believer can trust in the Lord's direction enthusiastically when we know the purpose behind the big questions—such as why world conditions get worse and worse before they get better. It is all for His glory and He is in control.
- In chapter seven, BUILDING YOUR SPIRITUAL BOMB SHELTER, I talked personally about faith building—how to make Christ as real in your life as an actual fortress.
- In chapter eight, WAITING-WATCHING-WORKING, I talked about the importance of an expectant attitude about Christ's return and how living a productive life in Him makes the waiting more rewarding.
- In chapter nine, OCCUPY UNTIL HE COMES, I am summarizing the main points of *Spiritual Prepping for the Rapture*. Are you ready to take up your marching orders?

I can think of no better way to reinforce the truths of this book than to quote the Word and let it speak for itself:

1 Timothy 6:11-15 – "But you, O man of God, flee these things and pursue righteousness, godliness, faith, love, patience, gentleness. Fight the good fight of faith, lay hold on eternal life, to which you were also called and have confessed the good confession in the presence of many witnesses... keep this commandment without spot, blameless until our Lord Jesus Christ's appearing, which He will manifest in His own time..."

The writing of the New Testament affirms again and again that the Church is to seek righteousness and to live in light of Christ's appearing. The life of the Church is staged on the backdrop of His imminent return. If the idea of living in expectation of His any moment return is still not significant in your thinking, let me present a final example.

THE MARRIAGE OF THE LAMB AND EXPECTANCY

The analogy of the Jewish wedding ceremony figures prominently in prophecy and reveals the importance of an expectant position regarding the Rapture. The Church *is* the Bride.

Revelation 19:6b-9—"'Alleluia! For the Lord God Omnipotent reigns! Let us be glad and rejoice and give Him glory, for the marriage of the Lamb has come, and His wife has made herself ready.' And to her it was granted to be arrayed in fine linen, clean and bright, for the fine linen is the righteous acts of the saints. Then he said to me, 'Write: 'Blessed are those who are called to the marriage supper of the Lamb!'"

Christ returns to claim His Bride, the Church, at the Rapture. Notice that the Bride or wife, the true Church, has made herself ready. Following the Rapture and during the Tribulation, the festivities of the wedding begin in heaven as mentioned earlier. The Bride is comprised of those He spoke of in John 17:9-12, those the Father gifted to the Son, like a father choosing a future wife for his son. When Christ returns to the earth at the end of the Tribulation the bride, who is now the wife of Christ, returns with Him. We, the Church Age remnant, shall return with Him. The wedding supper continues in the thousand-year Millennial Kingdom and the resurrected Old Testament Saints and Tribulation Saints, both living and resurrected, are those who are guests called to the marriage supper of the Lamb. The Saints of all the ages celebrate together.

In a contemporary American wedding ceremony, the bride and groom set a date and often send out "save the date" cards so that those who will be invited mark the event ahead of time. This was not the case in Jewish wedding ceremonies in Jesus' day. A date was not set for the wedding. In general, the bridegroom would show up to claim his bride about a year after the betrothal or when both were of age. But the day and the hour was not known. The bride was to be prepared for whenever the groom's friend went before him shouting "behold the bridegroom cometh." Her maids would quickly put on their wedding garments, go to her home and then adorn her to meet the bridegroom. Everything would be laid out in preparation because she did not know the exact time he would appear.

Anyone who missed the announcement of the groom's coming and did not go out to meet him or did not have a wedding garment would not be allowed into the wedding feast.

The bridegroom expected to find his bride dressed in her very best and ready to leave her childhood home for his own. Just because she did not know the exact day did not prevent her from being ready. She had to be fully-prepared ahead of the time. How will Christ view a bride who is not excited enough about her wedding to live in a state of constant preparedness and anticipation? Will they hear "well done?"

We cannot treat the Rapture as irrelevant just because we cannot know the day or hour. It may *not* happen in our life time but the point is it *could* happen in our life time. In fact, our Lord commands us to watch to make it clear we must assume it is near, even at the door.

Because the Lord said we cannot know, some believers assume that studying the signs and preparing spiritually falls into the category of date setting. After all, they surmise, we cannot know. The Lord emphasized that we cannot know the day or the hour because if we did, we definitely would *not* live in anticipation. It is human nature to put off today what we can deal with tomorrow, which is why we cannot know. Christ wants our minds to be constantly occupied with Him and His business and His return, not on our own pursuits. The only way to ensure constant readiness is to allow the Church of all times to live as if the Rapture could happen in their lifetime. It is the attitude of expectation that He desires in order to abide in Him. That is what He expects during the entire duration of the Church Age.

PETER'S VISUAL AID OF LIVING FAITH AND HOPE

Let me share a final example of how to live faith and hope that may help you put spiritual prepping in shoe leather. It comes from a favorite Sunday school lesson in Matthew 14:22-33 – Peter walking on the water.

Peter saw the ethereal form of Christ walking on the water toward the disciples' boat on the Sea of Galilee. In his need to reach and touch his Lord in the violent storm, he asked to walk to Him on the water. Perhaps there was that germ of emotional pride that also caused him to put one foot in front of the other. But Christ said "Come." Peter walked on the water until he was distracted by the high winds and the stormy waves. The moment he took his eyes from Jesus and put them on his circumstances, he went under.

Jesus is calling all of us to walk on water in this temporal life. We are to walk through the fire, the storms, and the dark valleys as if there is no fire, water or darkness. He does not promise to take away the storm; but as long as we keep our eyes on Him and not on our own ability, He promises to direct our paths and make even trials turn out for the good [Proverbs 3:5; Romans 8:28]. This is the kind of faith He expects of His Bride.

My son knows I am intimidated by water hazards on the golf course. As I prepare to hit the ball he reminds me to hit it as if there is no water. Because I have heard my ball make that plunking noise so many times, I have a difficult time doing that. But he is right. I have to focus on the green, not the water. It is the same with hope and faith. My husband said in basic training they were taught to trust their training and their trainer. Our combat trainer is Jesus Christ. We can trust Him completely. Our times are in His hands. We can rest in the Lord and wait patiently for Him [Psalm 31:15; 37:7]…and walk on water in the meantime.

In praying I like to ask the Lord to shine a bright light on the paths I am to take, strong enough so that I can see them clearly. Preppers know the value of a good flashlight or lantern with plenty of extra batteries. Christ is the light of the world; He never runs out of power. I need to remind myself that I am not operating on my own ability; I am operating on His.

I would like to say I have learned all the lessons I am sharing with you but my education and sanctification will continue until He takes me home. In college my professors would make sure we were listening to lectures by saying, "You will be tested on this." Yes, we are tested again and again and we will fail more than one test before we finally get it. Peter needed that plunge into cold water so he could feel the strong arm of Jesus reaching down to pull him up. We need that same reminder. Christ will never leave us and is always there to pull us up.

CLOSING WORDS

There are spiritual topics that seem stale because we are preaching to the choir but it is often the choir that is the most resistant. The claim is made that prophetic scripture isn't important because it has nothing to do with salvation. We *are* saved by grace through faith in Jesus Christ alone. But if we are saved by Christ's grace through faith in Christ, shouldn't we be concerned about learning everything we can about Christ? Studying Revelation and other prophecy is not a pre-requisite for salvation. But salvation should give us a desire to read the book of His full revealing; our salvation should cause us to long for His appearing. Listen to Paul's words to the Church at Corinth:

1 Corinthians 1:4-8—"I thank my God always concerning you for the grace of God which was given to you by Christ Jesus, that you were enriched in everything by Him in all utterance and all knowledge, even as the testimony of Christ was confirmed in you, so that you come short in no gift, eagerly waiting for the revelation of our Lord Jesus Christ, who will also confirm you to the end, that you may be blameless in the day of our Lord Jesus Christ."

Notice that the grace given to us in Christ Jesus that leads to salvation is not separated from the eager waiting for His revealing. The day of our Lord Jesus Christ is the special title of the Rapture/Resurrection of the Church. All that we do in Christ is done in light of the imminent return of Christ so that when He comes He finds us blameless. In addition to urging you to live an expectant faith and hope in Christ, let me leave you with two take-away truths:

- *The answer to every spiritual question is = for the glory of God.*
- *The answer to every problem is = to draw closer [abide] to Christ.*

Embracing these truths is your spiritual survival for the end of the end times. Don't miss the blessing of living an expectant life. It is like walking down new paths to exciting destinations. Expectancy can be your constant companion. The return of our Lord Jesus is just the beginning, not the end. All you have to do is leave the gate open.

Revelation 22:20—"He who testifies to these things says, 'Surely I am coming quickly.' Amen. Even so, come, Lord Jesus!"

~

Epilogue

If you are not a true believer in Jesus Christ, you will gain little from reading this book. Some practical information may be useful but the secret of end times survival is applicable only to the spiritually born again. The natural man cannot understand spiritual truth. [1 Corinthians 2:14]

If you have a desire to follow Christ but have not yet come to Him, He is waiting for you. "All that the Father gives Me will come to Me, and the one who comes to Me I will by no means cast out." [John 6:37] Are you ready to respond to His call?

- Confess that you are a sinner in need of the Savior. [Romans 3:10] Those who do not view themselves as lost cannot be found.
- Understand that you cannot save yourself; all fall short of the glory of God. We don't have it in us... [Romans 3:23]
- Death is the natural path of sinners. [Romans 6:23] Turn around and choose life.
- The solution is to believe in the Lord Jesus Christ, the one who died for your sins and rose from the dead. [Romans 10:9-10; 1 Corinthians 15:1-11; Ephesians 2:8-10] Faith in Christ, not works, is the only way to salvation.
- Come all the way to Christ by submitting to Him and letting go of your own way. [James 2:19; John 14:6]
- If you made this decision by faith, you are no longer under the judgment of death; Christ has raised you from spiritual death through His own

death on the cross and His resurrection. You have been born again to a living hope and newness of life. [Romans 8:1; 6:4]

Eternal salvation is a life or death decision. When the Titanic sank in frigid waters, many in First Class survived because they had a life boat. Steerage passengers were not so fortunate. Do not go down with the ship. Spend eternity with Christ.

~

www.ingramcontent.com/pod-product-compliance
Lightning Source LLC
Chambersburg PA
CBHW051043030426
42339CB00006B/162